SPANISH GRAMMAR
Your Guide

Fifth edition

Andrew Anderson

in association with

Val Levick

Glenise Radford

Alasdair McKeane

MALVERN LANGUAGE GUIDES
MLG

CONTENTS

Abbreviations

*	see note below
**	see second note below
§	see note below
†	see note below
(*m*)	masculine
(*f*)	feminine
(*pl*)	plural
ms	masculine singular
mpl	masculine plural
fs	feminine singular
fpl	feminine plural

Verb Table pages 103-107 contains common irregular verbs

GRAMMATICAL TERMS EXPLAINED

Grammatical terms are frequently thought of as boring and/or confusing, but, in reality, they need be neither. Once you have sorted out in your mind what they mean and what they do, you will realise that they are helpful, user-friendly tools for you to employ in your language learning.
In this list you will find, arranged in alphabetical order, some of the terms you are likely to meet.

ADJECTIVES (LOS ADJETIVOS):

These are words which describe or tell you more about a noun.
There are many kinds of adjectives: *big, blue, intelligent, Spanish* but they all serve to give extra information about their noun.

ADVERBS (LOS ADVERBIOS):

These are words which are added to a verb, adjective or another adverb to tell you how, when, where (*quickly, soon, there*) a thing was done.

Two "technical terms" that you will encounter with both adjectives and adverbs are **Comparative (Comparativo)** and **Superlative (Superlativo)**.

Comparative is the form of the adjective used to say that someone or something is *bigger/quicker/more intelligent,* etc than someone or something else.

Superlative is the form of the adjective used for saying that someone or something is *best, worst, biggest, most intelligent,* etc.

AGREEMENT (LA CONCORDANCIA):

This is the word used for the way in which adjectives change their spelling to agree with (match) the noun they are describing, or the way a verb changes to agree with its subject. Past participles may also show agreement in the passive form of the verb.

ARTICLES (LOS ARTÍCULOS):

There are three kinds of articles:

Definite (El artículo definido/determinado): *the*
Indefinite (El artículo indefinido/indeterminado): *a, an, some*
The "lo" article (El artículo "lo")

CLAUSES (LAS CLÁUSULAS):

These are parts of a sentence which contain a subject and a verb which agrees with that subject: In the sentence: "I said *that he should do it."* the italicised phrase is the clause.

CONJUNCTIONS (LAS CONJUNCIONES):

These are words used to join words, phrases, clauses and sentences: eg *and, but, for, or, when, while.*

GENDER (EL GÉNERO):

There are two genders in Spanish: masculine and feminine. All nouns fit into one or other of these categories: **el chico/la chica** *the boy/girl*, **el árbol** (m) *tree*, **la flor** (f) *flower.*

NOUNS (LOS SUSTANTIVOS):

These are names of people, places and things.

They can be	either	**common (común):** *boy, girl, bike, house*
	or	**proper (propio):** *Madrid, Francisco*
	and either	**abstract (abstracto):** *kindness, anger, justice,*
	or	**concrete (concreto):** *table, rabbit, car*

NUMBER (EL NÚMERO):

Things can be: **singular (singular):** *one only*
plural (plural): *two or more*

PREPOSITIONS (LAS PREPOSICIONES):

These are words placed in front of nouns and pronouns to show position and other relationships:

in *the garden*	***between*** *the houses*	***on*** *the floor*
before *midnight*	***after*** *8 o'clock*	***around*** *teatime*

PRONOUNS (LOS PRONOMBRES):

Pronouns fall into one of the following categories:

1. **Demonstrative (Demostrativos):**
   These pronouns are used to differentiate between: *this/that*, *these/those*

2. **Direct Object (de Complemento Directo):**
   These show who or what is the recipient of the verb action:
   me, you, him, her, it, us, them
   Example: *I see **you***

3. **Indirect Object (de Complemento Indirecto):**
   These are: *to me, to you, to him/her/it, to us, to them*
   Example: *I give it **to you***

4. **Indefinite (Indefinidos/Indeterminados):**
   These can be either the subject or the object of the verb.
   Example: *each one, someone, everything*

5. **Interrogative (Interrogativos):**
   These pronouns ask questions:
   Example: *Who?*

6. **Personal (Personales):**

   This is the general name given to subject, direct object, indirect object, and reflexive pronouns:

They can be	first person	*I, me, we, us*
	second person	*you*
	third person	*he, him, she, her, they, them*

7. **Possessive (Posesivos):**

   These pronouns signify ownership:

   mine, yours, his, hers, ours, theirs

8. **Prepositional (Preposicionales):**

   These are a strong form of the pronoun used after a preposition or for emphasis where, in English, we would show emphasis with the voice:

   Example: *with **me*** *for **us*** ***You** can't see him*

9. **Reflexive (Reflexivos):**

   These object pronouns refer back to the subject of the verb:

   myself, yourself, himself, herself, ourselves, yourselves, themselves

10. **Relative (Relativos)**:

    These pronouns introduce a clause giving more information about a noun:

    who, whom, which, that, whose

11. **Subject (de Sujeto):**

    These pronouns show who is performing the action of the verb:

    I, you, he, she, it, one, we, you, they

VERBS (LOS VERBOS):

Some pupils may think that Spanish verbs are difficult, but **if** you are prepared to give time to learning them thoroughly, you will find that even the irregular verbs follow certain patterns and that they are a valuable tool when speaking and writing the language.
A verb will tell you the actions and events in a sentence.

Example: **Juego** al fútbol ***I am playing** football*
Él llegó a la casa ***He arrived** at the house*
Mirábamos la televisión ***We were watching** TV*

There are some "technical" words which are used when talking about verbs.

Infinitive (El Infinitivo):

This is the "name" of the verb and it is the form which is listed in a dictionary or verb table. It means "to ..."

Example: **mirar** - ***to** look at, **to** watch*

The final two letters of the Spanish infinitive are very important. They will tell you which group or "family" the verb belongs to.

Conjugation (La Conjugación):

This is the term used to enumerate the different forms, tenses, moods and persons of the verb. It is the name given to the pattern which verbs follow.
There are three conjugations in Spanish, which are identified by the final two letters of the infinitive: **-ar, -er,** and **-ir**, as, for example, in the verbs baj**ar**, corr**er**, part**ir**.
All Spanish verbs belong to one or other of these basic groups; each group has its own characteristic regular pattern, but each group also has some verbs that are irregular.

Radical Changing Verbs (Los Verbos de Raíz Variable):

These verbs are neither entirely regular nor entirely irregular. "Radical" refers to the "root" or "stem" of the verb: in certain tenses, moods or persons the vowel in the root changes, following fairly predictable rules. These verbs exist in all three conjugations.

Example:	**mostrar** *to show*	**muestro** *I show*	but	**mostraron** *they showed*
	pedir *to request*	**pidieron** *they requested*	but	**pedimos** *we request*

Other Irregular Verbs (Los Verbos Irregulares):

These verbs, which do not follow one of the three regular patterns, are set out for you in the Verb Table at the back of the book. They are verbs which are frequently used and which you **must** know, for example: **ir** *to go,* **ser** *to be,* **decir** *to say*

Object (El Complemento):

This is the person or thing affected by the action of the verb.
The object of the sentence can be either a noun or a pronoun:

Example:	Comemos **las manzanas**	*We eat **the apples***
	Los vemos	*We see **them***

Reflexive Verbs (Los Verbos Reflexivos):

These are verbs which have an extra pronoun. Example: **Me** acuesto *I go to bed*
These verbs are used to convey several types of ideas:

a) a truly reflexive action in which the subject performs the action to/for him/herself:
Example: **Nos** lavamos *We wash **ourselves***

b) a reciprocal action in which the subjects perform the action to/for each other:
Example: **Se** miran *They look at **each other***

c) an action considered reflexive in Spanish, although not necessarily so in English:
Example: El niño **se** duerme *The child falls asleep*

d) they are used to avoid using the Passive:
Example: El gazpacho **se come** en Andalucía *"Gazpacho" **is eaten** in Andalusia*

Subject (El Sujeto):

This is the person or thing performing the action of the verb.
The subject can be either a noun or a pronoun:

Example: **Las muchachas** ven un perro. **Ellas** le dan algo de comer
***The girls** see a dog. **They** give it something to eat*

Tenses (Los Tiempos):

Tenses are the methods by which verbs tell you **when** events take place, will take place, took place, used to take place, etc. The names of the tenses are a guide to their use:
- the **Present (el Presente)** tells you what *is happening now,* or what *usually happens*
- the **Future (el Futuro)** tells you what *will happen*
- the **Conditional (el Potencial Simple)** tells you what *would happen*
- the **Preterite (el Pretérito Indefinido)** tells you what *happened* in the past
- the **Imperfect (el Pretérito Imperfecto)** tells you what *was happening* in the past

Past Participles (Los Participios Pasados/de Pretérito):

Past Participles are parts of a verb used with the **auxiliary verb (verbo auxiliar)** (in Spanish the verb is **haber**) to form **Compound** tenses:
- the **Perfect (Pretérito Perfecto)** tells you what *has happened*
- the **Pluperfect (Pretérito Pluscuamperfecto)** tells you what *had happened*

In English, Past Participles often end in **-en, -ed** or **-t**: *giv**en**, look**ed**, bought*
In Spanish, regular Past Participles end in **-ado** (infinitive **-ar**) or **-ido** (infinitive **-er** and **-ir**)
    Example: and**ado**, corr**ido**, part**ido**
Several verbs have irregular past participles which need to be learned carefully.

Gerund (El Gerundio):

This is a part of the verb which ends in **-ing** in English, and **-ando** (infinitive **-ar**) or **-iendo** (infinitive **-er**/**-ir**) in Spanish. English gerunds are often translated by the Spanish infinitive.
    Example: Me gusta **ir** al cine   *I like **going** (to go) to the cinema*
In Spanish the gerund, which is invariable, is used with the auxiliary verb *estar* to form what are called the **Progressive Tenses (Tiempos Progresivos)**.
    Example: Estoy cocin**ando**   *I am cooking*   Estaba llov**iendo**   *It was raining*

Present Participle (El Participio de Presente):

This is a part of the verb which ends in **-ing** in English, and **-ante**/**-ente**/**-iente** in Spanish. English present participles combine with the auxiliary verb *to be* to create the continuous or progressive tenses. Many Spanish verbs do not form present participles at all; when they do, the resulting form normally functions as an adjective or a noun.
    Example: platillos vol**antes**   *fly**ing** saucers*

Imperatives or **Commands (El Imperativo):**

These are the forms of the verb you use when telling somebody (including yourself) to do something. Example: **¡Salta!** *Jump!*   **¡Saltemos!** *Let's jump!*   **¡Saltad!** *Jump!*

Active or **Passive (La Voz Activa** o **Pasiva):**

Verbs can be either active or passive:
Active means that the subject performs the action on or for the object:
    Example: Ella **perdió** al gato en el jardín   *She **lost** the cat in the garden*
Passive which means that the subject is the recipient of the action:
    Example: El gato **ha sido encontrado** en el árbol *The cat **has been found** in the tree*

ACCENTS (LOS ACENTOS)

Accents are not decorative in Spanish, nor are they arbitrary. They are functional, and should not be thought of as an "optional extra". You should get into the habit of writing them as you write the letter of the word over which they appear.

There are three standard accents in Spanish:

the acute " ´ " the dieresis " ¨ " and the tilde " ˜ "

The tilde is only ever found over the letter "n" in Spanish, and so n-tilde "ñ" should be thought of as a separate letter of the alphabet. The acute is by far the most commonly occurring accent.

Accents in Spanish serve several different purposes:

They show you how to pronounce words.
They preserve the same stress in different forms of the same word.
They differentiate between different meanings or uses of the same word.

1. Spanish has a simple set of standard rules regarding stress and pronunciation: Words ending in a vowel, "n" or "s" have the stress on the penultimate (next-to-last) syllable.

Example:	la herm**a**na *sister*	el ch**i**co *boy*
	j**o**ven *young*	l**u**nes *Monday*

Words ending in all the other consonants have the stress on the last syllable.

Example:	trabaj**ar** *to work*	españ**o**l *Spanish*

2. However, some words in Spanish have a pronunciation at variance with these rules, and so a written acute accent is required to show the difference in stress.

Example:	el sof**á** (<u>not</u> el s***o***fa) *sofa*	el l**á**piz (<u>not</u> el lap***i***z) *pencil*

Note that all words in Spanish which have the stress on the antepenultimate syllable (last syllable but two) require the written accent to indicate this.

Example:	la br**ú**jula *compass*	el hipop**ó**tamo *hippopotamus*

3. Acute accents maintain the stress on the same syllable of a word in its singular and plural forms.

Example: joven *young* (stress on "o", no written accent required)
j**ó**venes (by the standard rule, the stress would fall on the -ve- syllable (jo-vE-nes), so now a written accent is required)

Similarly, acute accents are written on parts of the verb when, for instance, pronouns are attached to them, again to maintain the original stress.

Example:

dar *to give*	darlo *to give it*	d**á**rmelo *to give it to me*
dando *giving*	d**á**ndolo *giving it*	d**á**ndomelo *giving it to me*

The opposite is also true.

Example: el rev**é**s *back, setback*
(written acute accent required to show correct pronunciation)
los reveses
(stress now falls on correct syllable automatically (revEses), so no written acute accent is required)

Likewise: un portugu**é**s *a Portuguese man*
una portuguesa *a Portuguese woman*

Exception: written acute accents on adjectives are <u>not</u> affected when they are transformed into adverbs by the addition of **-mente**.

Example: f**á**cil → f**á**cilmente

4. Acute accents sometimes serve to differentiate between the meanings of words that are otherwise spelt and pronounced identically.

Example:

aun *even*	solo *alone*	el *the*	si *if*
a**ú**n *still*	s**ó**lo *only*	**é**l *he*	s**í** *yes*

More frequently, acute accents also function as a kind of flag to indicate that the same word is being used in a different grammatical function.

Example:

este hombre	*this man*	(demonstrative adjective)
éste	*this one* (*m*)	(demonstrative pronoun)

Cenaremos cuando venga (conjunction)
We'll have supper when he comes
¿Cu**á**ndo vendrá el correo? (interrogative)
When will the post come?

5. The dieresis is used to show that a vowel is clearly pronounced and not run into another vowel beside it.
For example, in Spanish "g" before "e" and "i" is pronounced as a jota ("j") sound; to make the "g" "hard", a "u" is inserted between the "g" and the "e/i".
If the "u" is to be pronounced separately from the "e/i", a dieresis then needs to be written over the "u".

Example: el germen *germ* ("g" pronounced as a "j")
la guerra *war* ("g" pronounced as hard "g", "u" not pronounced at all)
la ling**üí**stica *linguistics* (hard "g"; "u" and "i" both pronounced)

Note that with the vowels "a" and "o" there is no room for confusion and so the written accent is not required: eg guapo ("u" and "a" both pronounced).

ADJECTIVES (LOS ADJETIVOS)

Adjectives are words which are put with a noun to give you more information about it:

Example:	una casa	una casa **enorme**	*an enormous house*
	el perro	el **primer** perro **blanco**	*the first white dog*

WATCH YOUR AGREEMENTS! (¡CUIDADO CON LAS CONCORDANCIAS!)

Adjectives in Spanish alter their spelling to **agree with** (match) the noun to which they are attached. Adjectives have a number of different methods of showing agreement:

1. A great many adjectives in Spanish end in **-o**; these change to **-a** to make the feminine form and add **-s** to make the plural:

	Masculine Singular	**Feminine Singular**	**Masculine Plural**	**Feminine Plural**	**Meaning**
Example:	pequeñ**o**	pequeñ**a**	pequeñ**os**	pequeñ**as**	*small, little*

2. If the adjective ends in **-a**, **-e**, **-í** or **-ú**, the feminine singular form is unchanged; **-s** is added to **-a** and **-e**, and **-es** is added to **-í** and **-ú**, to create both masculine and feminine plurals:

	ms	**fs**	**mpl**	**fpl**	**Meaning**
Example:	verde	verde	verde**s**	verde**s**	*green*
	baladí	baladí	baladí**es**	baladí**es**	*trivial*

3. In many cases, if the adjective ends in a consonant, the feminine singular form is again unchanged, and **-es** is added to create both masculine and feminine plurals:

	ms	**fs**	**mpl**	**fpl**	**Meaning**
Example:	azul	azul	azul**es**	azul**es**	*blue*
	auxiliar	auxiliar	auxiliar**es**	auxiliar**es**	*auxiliary*
	gris	gris	gris**es**	gris**es**	*grey*

(Note: in the plural, j**ó**venes acquires an accent to maintain the same stress; also, a final **-z** changes to **-c-** before **-es**.)

joven	joven	jóven**es**	jóven**es**	*young*
capaz	capaz	capa**ces**	capa**ces**	*capable*

Unfortunately, there are a number of exceptions to these three basic rules.

4. If the adjective ends in **-án**, **-ín**, **-ón**, **-or**, **-és**, **-ete** or **-ote**, then a distinct feminine form is created with **-a** (plural **-as**), and masculine plural with **-es**:

	ms	**fs**	**mpl**	**fpl**	**Meaning**
Example:	malandrín	malandrin**a**	malandrin**es**	malandrin**as**	*malign*
	bonachón	bonachon**a**	bonachon**es**	bonachon**as**	*good-natured*
	encantador	encantador**a**	encantador**es**	encantador**as**	*charming*
	grandote	grandot**a**	grandote**s**	grandot**as**	*very big*

Exception: adjectives of *comparison* ending in **-or**, eg **mayor, peor, inferior** and **anterior** do **not** have a distinct feminine form.

5. Most adjectives of region and nationality agree in both gender and number. This holds true of words ending in **-o**, **-án** and **-és**, as one would expect, but also of words ending in **-l** and **-z**:

	ms	fs	mpl	fpl	Meaning
Example:	británic**o**	británic**a**	británic**os**	británic**as**	*British*
	alem**án**	aleman**a**	aleman**es**	aleman**as**	*German*
	franc**és**	frances**a**	frances**es**	frances**as**	*French*
	españo**l**	español**a**	español**es**	español**as**	*Spanish*
	andaluz	andaluz**a**	andalu**ces**	andaluz**as**	*Andalusian*

However, as illustrated in point 2 above, certain adjectives of nationality (those ending in **-a**, **-e**, **í**, **ú**, **-al** and **-ar**) do <u>not</u> have separate feminine forms:

	ms	fs	mpl	fpl	Meaning
Example:	belga	belga	belga**s**	belga**s**	*Belgian*
	canadiense	canadiense	canadiense**s**	canadiense**s**	*Canadian*
	israelí	israelí	israelí**es**	israelí**es**	*Israeli*

6. A few adjectives are completely invariable: eg **cada**. Although Spanish has some "normal" adjectives of colour (amarillo, rojo, etc), many colours are rendered with the phrase **color**, **color de** or **de color** plus a noun. This phrase often falls away, leaving the noun alone which then functions like an invariable adjective.

Example:	ojos **color de violeta**	*violet(-coloured) eyes*
	bufandas **naranja**	*orange scarves*
	azulejos **turquesa**	*turquoise tiles*

7. Compound adjectives of colour are invariable:

Example:	una falda **azul marino/azul claro**	*a navy blue/light blue skirt*
	un jersey **azul marino/azul claro**	*a navy blue/light blue pullover*
	unos pantalones **marrón oscuro**	*a dark brown pair of trousers*

8. Some shades of colour are rendered by compound adjectives which agree with the noun in a normal fashion:

Example:	una botella **verdinegra**	*a very dark green bottle*
	dos taxis **blanquinegros**	*two black-and-white taxis*

Other compound adjectives function in the same way:

Example:	**pelirrubio, -a, -os, -as**	*fair-haired*
	socioeconómico, -a, -os, -as	*socioeconomic*

9. Most cardinal numbers are also invariable. However, **uno** (**un**) and numbers for 200-900 formed with **-cientos** <u>do</u> agree in gender:

Example:	un coche	*one/a car*	una botella	*one/a bottle*
	doscientos dólares	*200 dollars*	quinientas libras	*500 pounds*

10. Several common adjectives have a shortened form which occurs in certain situations. This phenomenon of shortening (losing the final syllable) is called **apocopation**. It always occurs when the adjective precedes the noun and always when the adjective and the corresponding noun are in the singular.

a) The cardinal number **uno** and the adjectives **alguno**, **ninguno**, **bueno**, **malo**, **primero**, **tercero** and **postrero** lose their final **-o** when they immediately precede a masculine singular noun; **ciento** loses its final **-to**. This does **not** affect their regular forms in the feminine and the plural.

Example:	el *primer* día, los **primeros** días	*the first day, the first days*
	algún dinero, **algunas** monedas	*some money, some coins*

Note that **alguno** and **ninguno** require an accent on the **-ú-** to preserve the stress.

b) **Grande** is shortened to **gran** before singular nouns of either gender if it precedes them. (**Grande** changes its meaning according to whether it precedes or follows the noun it is qualifying; this is dealt with in point 7 on page 12.)

Example:	un **gran** éxito, una **gran** tragedia	*a great success, a great tragedy*
	los **grandes** países, **grandes** damas	*the great countries, great ladies*

c) **Santo** is shortened to **San** before masculine proper names, unless the name begins with **Do**- or **To**-. However, when **santo** means *holy, blessed* and not *saint* it acts as a normal adjective.

Example:	**San** Juan, **San** Pedro, **San** Miguel **but**	**Santo** Domingo, **Santo** Tomás
	la **santa** Iglesia católica	*the Holy Catholic Church*
	todo el **santo** día	*the whole blessed day*

11. When one adjective is combined with two or more masculine nouns (either singular, plural or a combination thereof), the adjective takes its masculine plural form:

Example:	el botón y el zapato perdid**os**	*the lost button and shoe*
	el profesor y los alumnos extranjer**os**	*the foreign teacher and pupils*
	gatos y perros simpátic**os**	*friendly cats and dogs*

Likewise, when one adjective is combined with two or more feminine nouns (either singular, plural or a combination thereof), it takes its feminine plural form:

Example:	dos manzanas y una pera madur**as**	*two ripe apples and a ripe pear*

However, when one adjective qualifies two or more nouns of **both genders (**either singular, plural or a combination thereof), the adjective takes the masculine plural form (regardless of the gender of the noun it is nearest):

Example:	un hombre y una mujer escoces**es**	*a Scottish man and woman*
	las tazas y el plato limpi**os**	*the clean cups and plate*
	los niños y las niñas travies**os**	*the mischievous boys and girls*

12. When two or more adjectives are combined with one plural noun, normally the meaning of all the adjectives is applied to that noun.

Hence **las noches largas y oscuras** *the long, dark nights*
means that **all** the nights are **both** long and dark.

However, if the noun is in the plural because there are several adjectives which are **each** qualifying **single** instances of that noun, then the adjectives go in the singular:

Example:	los equipos vencedor y derrotado	*the winning and the losing teams*

In this example there is **one** winning team and **one** losing team.
But note that: los equipos vencedor**es** y derrotad**os**
would mean *the winning teams and the losing teams*

13. Adjectives themselves may have additional words - adverbs - put with them to add to, refine or alter their meaning:

Example:	**caro**	*expensive*
	más caro	*more expensive*
	menos caro	*less expensive*
	muy caro	*very expensive*
	demasiado caro	*too expensive*
	tan caro	*so expensive*
	cada vez más caro	*more and more expensive*
	cada vez menos caro	*less and less expensive*
	bastante caro	*fairly/rather expensive*
	sumamente caro	*extremely expensive*

14. Some adjectives add a prefix (an extra syllable at the front) to change their meaning to the opposite of the original. However, it should be noted that in numerous cases Spanish does not have the corresponding opposite form:

Example:	contento	*happy*	**des**contento	***un**happy*
	posible	*possible*	**im**posible	***im**possible*
	creíble	*credible*	**in**creíble	***in**credible*
but:	importante	*important*	**poco** importante	***un**important*
	manchado	*stained*	**sin** manchas	***un**stained*

POSITION OF ADJECTIVES (¿DÓNDE PONER LOS ADJETIVOS?)

1. Most adjectives create a category of the person or thing described and differentiate them from others. This kind of adjective **always follows** the noun:

   Example: Lleva una camisa **blanca** y una corbata **roja**
   He is wearing a white shirt and a red tie

   White shirts are a category of **all** shirts; **white** shirts are different from **blue** shirts.

   Conduce un coche **francés** *He drives a French car*

   French cars are a category of the world-wide production of cars.

2. Adjectives that do not create a category can **either** precede **or** follow the noun:

   Example:

Luchó en la **sangrienta** batalla	*He fought in the bloody battle*
La puesta del sol en el **lejano** horizonte	*The sunset on the distant horizon*

   Note: Most or all battles are generally bloody; "**la batalla sangrienta**" would tend to imply that some other battles being referred to were not bloody or were less bloody than the one in which he participated. The adjective "**lejano**" is subjective - the horizon **seems** distant to the viewer and by definition there is only one horizon.

3. Several common adjectives are **always** placed **before** the noun:

   mucho, **poco**, **otro**, **tanto**, **demasiado**, **tal**, **cada**, **todo**, **ambos**, **último**, **mero**, **cualquier**, **llamado** (*so-called*), and cardinal and ordinal numbers:

Example:	Tengo **demasiadas** tareas	*I have too many tasks*
	todos los otros parientes	*all the other relatives*
	tantos primeros premios	*so many first prizes*

4. A few common adjectives are quite frequently encountered **before** the noun, though when they clearly differentiate, they will still **follow** the noun:

Example:	¡**Buenos** días!	*Good morning, good afternoon!*
	la **mala** suerte	*hard luck, bad luck*
	un **pequeño** pájaro cantaba	*a small bird was singing*
but:	Prefiero el vaso **pequeño**	*I prefer the small glass*

5. When you have a noun described by two adjectives, they will both take up their normal position:

Example:	**muchos llamados** expertos	*many so-called experts*
	pocos amigos **verdaderos**	*few true friends*

6. If you are using two adjectives which follow the noun and which apply to it equally, they should be linked by the word **y**. If there are more than two adjectives, only the final two are linked by **y**.

Example: unas alumnas **inteligentes y trabajadoras**
intelligent, hard-working pupils
unas alumnas **inteligentes, animadas y trabajadoras**
intelligent, lively, hard-working pupils

However, if a second adjective further qualifies a "core phrase" already made up of a noun + adjective combination, **y** is not required:

Example: los problemas sociales americanos *American social problems*
("Social problems" is the core phrase; American social problems are only a sub-group of global social problems.)

7. There are some adjectives whose meaning changes according to whether they are put **before** or **after** the noun:

adjective	***meaning before the noun***	***meaning after the noun***
antiguo	*former, ex-*	*old, old-fashioned, antique*
cierto	*certain, some, unspecified*	*indubitable, sure, correct*
diferentes	*different (sundry), various, several*	*different (from one another)*
distintos	*different (sundry), various, several*	*different (from one another)*
grande	*great*	*big, tall*
medio	*half (a/an, of), mid-*	*average, middle*
mismo	*(the) same*	*very, selfsame, -self*
nuevo	*new (fresh), another, further, renewed*	*new (brand new)*
pobre	*poor, wretched (to be pitied)*	*poor (needy, impoverished)*
puro	*sheer, plain, simple*	*pure, clean, untainted*
raro	*rare, scarce, infrequent*	*strange, odd*
simple	*simple (mere); single*	*simple-minded*
único	*only, sole*	*unique*
varios	*several*	*assorted, mixed, varied*
viejo	*long-standing, previous (one before)*	*old, aged*

Example:

A **media** mañana yo **mismo** hice **nuevos** esfuerzos de hablar con el **antiguo** dueño
*In **mid**-morning I **myself** made **new** efforts to speak with the **former** owner*
El precio **medio** de los muebles **nuevos** y **antiguos** ha subido al **mismo** nivel
*The **average** price of **new** and **antique** furniture has risen to the **same** level*

Comparison Of Adjectives (La Comparación De Los Adjetivos)

Comparative Adjectives (Adjetivos Comparativos)

To say that something is newer, more powerful, more expensive, etc, you put **más** in front of the adjective; the resulting phrase almost always follows the noun it is qualifying.

Example: Tengo un coche **más grande**, pero ella tiene un coche **más rápido**
I have a bigger car but she has a faster car

To compare one thing with another you use:

más ... que	*more ... than*
menos ... que	*less ... than*
tan ... como	*as ... as*

You must be careful to make the adjective agree as normal:

Example: Mi hermano es **más** alt**o** **que** mi hermana
My brother is taller than my sister
Mi hermana es **menos** terc**a** **que** mi hermano
My sister is less stubborn than my brother
Mi madre es **tan** activ**a** **como** mi padre
My mother is as active as my father

Four very common adjectives have irregular comparative forms:

bueno *good* becomes **mejor** *better* **malo** *bad* becomes **peor** *worse*

Example: Mick tiene una **buena** idea, pero Val tiene una idea **mejor**
Mick has a good idea, but Val has a better one
Esta película es **mala**, pero la otra es **peor**
This film is bad, but the other one is worse

grande *great, big* has two comparative forms: **mayor** and **más grande**
mayor is used for importance or age; **más grande** is used for size

Example: Soy **mayor** que mi amigo y por eso me toca el trozo **más grande**
I am older than my friend and so the bigger piece is for me
Esta reforma va a tener **mayor** impacto en la sociedad
This reform is going to have a greater impact on society

pequeño *small* also has two comparative forms: **menor** and **más pequeño**
menor is used for importance or age; **más pequeño** is used for size

Example: Mi hermana **menor** es **más pequeña** que yo
My younger sister is smaller than I am
Los títulos de nobleza tienen **menor** valor en la sociedad de hoy
Titles of nobility have less value in today's society

Superlative Adjectives (Los Adjetivos Superlativos)

Superlative adjectives - *the biggest, strongest, most useful* - are not visibly different from comparative adjectives in Spanish, and so much of the differentiation of meaning comes from the context in which they are used. The definite article - **el**, **la** - often, but not always, signals the superlative form.

Compare:	Este florero es más bonito *This vase is **prettier***	with	Este florero es **el** más bonito *This vase is **the prettiest***

Also compare Tomaremos **el** tren más rápido para viajar a Madrid
*We shall take the fast**est** train to travel to Madrid (of several alternatives)*
with Entre el AVE y el TALGO, escogimos **el** tren más rápido
*Between the AVE and the TALGO, we chose the fast**er** train*
(AVE and TALGO are two different types of Spanish train)

The irregular comparative forms - **mejor**, **peor**, **mayor**, **menor** - follow the same rules:

Example:	El **mejor** alumno	*The best pupil*
	La **mejor** idea	*The best idea*
	Es él quien tiene la **peor** habitación	*He has the worst room*
	Lo **peor** de todo es que ...	*The worst of it all is that ...*

Mi familia tiene tres coches y el mío es el **peor**
My family has three cars and mine is the worst

Su primera tragicomedia fue su **mayor** fracaso
His first tragicomedy was his greatest failure
Eso no tiene la **menor** importancia
That hasn't the slightest importance

The "absolute superlative" does not create a real comparison but rather strengthens the force of the adjective to which it is applied.
In Spanish there are two ways of creating the absolute superlative: **muy** + adjective, and **-ísimo** added to the end of the adjective.

Example: esa canción es **muy** hermosa **or** esa canción es hermos**ísima**
that song is very/most beautiful

Care should be exercised with **-ísimo** as not all adjectives accept this suffix, and even when they do, numerous adjectives change their spelling when combining with the suffix.

Example:	rico	→	ri**qu**ísimo	largo	→	lar**gu**ísimo
	joven	→	joven**c**ísimo	feliz	→	feli**c**ísimo

In addition, there are many entirely irregular formations, including:

Example:	malo	→	pésimo	antiguo	→	antiquísimo

MORE ADJECTIVES (¡MÁS ADJETIVOS!)

There are several other types of adjectives that you may have to use.
They are: Possessive Adjectives, Demonstrative Adjectives, Interrogative Adjectives (including adjectives used in exclamations) and Indefinite Adjectives. Their names tell you the role they play in the sentence.

POSSESSIVE ADJECTIVES (LOS ADJETIVOS POSESIVOS)

These are the words you use with nouns to show ownership of an object.
In English they are *my, your, his, her, its, our, their*. In Spanish there are two sets of possessive: **mi**, **tu**, etc and **mío**, **tuyo**, etc.
The choice of possessives is mainly a matter of style, as in the following examples:

mi primo	***my** cousin*	un primo **mío**	*a cousin **of mine***
vuestras colegas	***your** colleagues*	unas colegas **vuestras**	*some colleagues **of yours***
una de **sus** características		una característica **suya**	
*one of **his** characteristics*		*a characteristic **of his***	

The first set always precedes the noun and the second set always follows the noun.
Both sets agree with the noun in number and, when they can, in gender.

The form of the adjective is determined according to the **gender of the thing owned** and <u>not</u> whether the owner is male or female! We **all** talk about **su** padre, **su** madre, **sus** hijos, and whether we mean *his*, *her* or *their* is established from the context.

The full list of the **normal** possessive adjectives is as follows:

	ms	**fs**	**mpl**	**fpl**	**Meaning**	
	one object owned		**several objects owned**			
one owner	mi	mi	mis	mis	*my*	**one owner**
	tu	tu	tus	tus	*your*	
	su	su	sus	sus	*his, her, its*	
2+ owners	nuestro	nuestra	nuestros	nuestras	*our*	**2+ owners**
	vuestro	vuestra	vuestros	vuestras	*your*	
	su	su	sus	sus	*their*	

The full list of the **alternative** possessive adjectives is as follows:

	ms	**fs**	**mpl**	**fpl**	**Meaning**	
	one object owned		**several objects owned**			
one owner	mío	mía	míos	mías	*mine*	**one owner**
	tuyo	tuya	tuyos	tuyas	*yours*	
	suyo	suya	suyos	suyas	*his, hers, its*	
2+ owners	nuestro	nuestra	nuestros	nuestras	*ours*	**2+ owners**
	vuestro	vuestra	vuestros	vuestras	*yours*	
	suyo	suya	suyos	suyas	*theirs*	

Remember:-

1. When using third person possessives, if the context is not clear and there is room for ambiguity, then the adjective can be replaced by an article and the phrases **de usted**, **de él**, **de ella**, **de ustedes**, **de ellos** or **de ellas** added after the noun:
   Example: Me gusta **su** parasol — *I like his/her/your/their sunshade*
   Me gusta el parasol **de Vd.** — *I like <u>your</u> sunshade*

2. When talking about parts of the body the article rather than the possessive adjective is used:
   Example: Ella abrió **los** ojos — *She opened **her** eyes*
   Levanté **el** brazo — *I raised **my** arm*
   With parts of the body and articles of clothing, the article is used plus an object pronoun with the verb:
   Example: Ellos **se** lavan las manos — *They wash **their** hands*
   Me puse el sombrero — *I put on **my** hat*
   Ella **le** enderezó la corbata — *She straightened **his** tie*
   Some verbs need a direct object pronoun, though again the article is used:
   Example: **Me** duele la cabeza — ***My** head hurts (me)*

3. The alternative possessive forms are employed in phrases of direct address:
   Example: Muy señores **míos** — *(**My**) Dear Sirs*
   Padre **nuestro** ... — ***Our** Father ...*
   They also are used frequently with the definite article and **lo**:
   Example: Éste es **el mío** — *This one is **mine***
   uno de **los nuestros** — *one of **ours** (our men, our family)*
   No me meto en **lo suyo** — *I don't get involved in **his affairs***

DEMONSTRATIVE ADJECTIVES (LOS ADJETIVOS DEMOSTRATIVOS)

These are the words you use to demonstrate or show which object you are describing. In English they are: *this, these; that, those*. In Spanish they are:

ms	**fs**	**mpl**	**fpl**	**meaning**
este	**esta**	**estos**	**estas**	*this, these*
ese	**esa**	**esos**	**esas**	*that, those (closer)*
aquel	**aquella**	**aquellos**	**aquellas**	*that, those (distant)*

Demonstratives precede the noun, and since they are adjectives, they agree in number and gender. Thus: **este** pájaro, **estas** rosas, **esa** casa, **esos** platos, **aquella** montaña, etc.

1. Notice that in Spanish there are **three** sets of demonstratives, as against two in English. While **este** corresponds closely to *this*, **ese** tends to refer to *that* closer to hand, and **aquel** to *that* further away in time or space:
   Example: ¿Prefieres **esta** motocicleta, **ese** coche o **aquel** camión?
   Do you prefer this motorbike (right beside us), that car (a few yards away) or that lorry over there (on the other side of the car park)?

2. You must also remember to repeat the correct adjective with each noun in a list:
   Example: ¿Dónde encontrase **este** zapato y **estos** calcetines?
   Where did you find this shoe and these socks?

INTERROGATIVE ADJECTIVES (LOS ADJETIVOS INTERROGATIVOS)

These are words which help you to ask questions about things.
In English we say *what? which? how much? how many?* In Spanish the words are:

ms	fs	mpl	fpl
¿qué?	**¿qué?**	**¿qué?**	**¿qué?**
¿cuál?	**¿cuál?**	**¿cuáles?**	**¿cuáles?**
¿cuánto?	**¿cuánta?**	**¿cuántos?**	**¿cuántas?**

Note that all these adjectives, as they are asking a question, require the written accent.
¿Qué? is the more general word for *what?* and it is invariable.
¿Cuál?, *which?*, is rarer and suggests a choice is being made out of a limited number of alternatives. **¿Cuál?** has a plural form which must agree with the noun.
¿Cuánto? means *how much?/how many?* and has to agree in number and gender.

Example:

¿**Qué** juegos te gustan? — ***What*** *games do you like?*
¿**Qué** programa estás mirando? — ***What*** *programme are you watching?*
¿**Cuál** pelota quieres, la roja o la amarilla? — ***Which*** *ball do you want, the red one or the yellow one?*
¿**Cuáles** manzanas prefieres? — ***Which*** *apples do you prefer?*
¿**Cuánto** dinero tienes? — ***How much*** *money do you have?*
¿**Cuántas** veces lo has dicho? — ***How many*** *times have you said so?*

These adjectives function in a similar way in indirect questions:

Example:

No sabíamos **qué** cosas había hecho
We didn't know ***what*** *things he had done*
No quiere decirnos **cuál** premio va a escoger
He doesn't want to tell us ***which*** *prize he is going to choose*
Intentábamos averiguar **cuántos** goles había marcado
We were trying to find out ***how many*** *goals he had scored*

It is worth noticing that **¡Qué!** is used in exclamations as well as in questions.
Note that Spanish never uses an article in these exclamations:

Example:

¡**Qué** lástima! — ***What*** *a pity!*
¡**Qué** idea! — ***The very*** *idea!*
¡**Qué** flores tan bellas/más bellas! — ***What*** *beautiful flowers!*

INDEFINITE ADJECTIVES (LOS ADJETIVOS INDEFINIDOS)

Here are some of the most common indefinite adjectives, with phrases to show you how they are used. Several of these have already been commented upon above.

Alguno, algún, alguna, algunos, algunas

Example:

alguna posibilidad — *some possibility*
algunos calamares — *some squid*

Cada (invariable)

Example:	**cada** día	*each day/every day*
	cada casa	*each house*

Cualquiera, cualquier, cualesquiera

Example: una hoja de papel **cualquiera**
any (old) sheet of paper

but: te agradecería **cualquier** ayuda
I would be thankful to you for any help whatsoever
unos tomates **cualesquiera**
any (old) tomatoes
(tomatoes which have been chosen entirely at random)

Tal, tales

Example: Nunca había considerado **tal** posibilidad
He had never considered such a possibility
Con **tal** ordenador sería fácil escribir muchos libros
It would be easy to write a lot of books with a computer like that
Tales animales son peligrosos
Such animals are dangerous

Notice: **tal** takes <u>no</u> indefinite article where we would say in English *such a ...*

Notice: you use **tal** if that is the only adjective, but **tan** if there are two or more adjectives:

Example: **tal** máquina
such a machine/a machine like that

but: un hombre **tan** orgulloso
such a proud man

Todo, toda, todos, todas

Example:	**todo** el bocadillo	*all the sandwich/the whole sandwich*
	todo el mundo	*everybody*
	toda la mañana	*all morning/the whole morning*
	todos los elefantes	*all (of) the elephants*
	todos los días	*every day*
	todas las muchachas	*all (of) the girls*

Notice: **todo**, etc **never** combines with **de** in these constructions, unlike the corresponding English form (*all <u>of</u>*).

Other common indefinite articles are:

ambos, -as	*both*	**ninguno, -ún, -a, -os, -as**	*no, any*
cierto, -a, -os, -as	*certain*	**otro, -a, -os, -as**	*other*
los/las demás	*the other*	**poco, -a, -os, -as**	*few*
demasiado, -a, -os, -as	*too much/many*	**tanto, -a, -os, -as**	*so much/many*
mismo, -a, -os, -as	*same*	**varios, -as**	*several*
mucho, -a, -os, -as	*many*		

ADVERBS (LOS ADVERBIOS)

Adverbs are words added to verbs, adjectives and other adverbs to tell you more about how, when, where a thing is/was/will be done.
Adverbs in English usually end in **-ly**; in Spanish they usually end in **-mente**:

El habla **cortésmente** *He speaks **politely*** Ella anda **lentamente** *She walks **slowly***

FORMATION OF ADVERBS (LA FORMACIÓN DE LOS ADVERBIOS)

1. Many adjectives end in **-o** (*m*) and **-a** (*f*); with these adjectives adverbs are created by using the feminine form as a basis and adding **-mente**:

	Masc Adj	**Fem Adj**	**Adverb**	**Meaning**
Example:	tranquilo	tranquila	tranquilamente	*calmly*

2. Some adjectives have a written accent; in these cases the accent is always retained when adding -**mente** to the feminine form to create the adverb:

	Masc Adj	**Fem Adj**	**Adverb**	**Meaning**
Example:	r**á**pido	r**á**pida	r**á**pidamente	*quickly*

3. Some adjectives in Spanish do not have different masculine and feminine endings; in these cases **-mente** is simply added to the adjective without any other change:

	Adj (Masc and Fem)	**Adverb**	**Meaning**
Example:	dulce	dulcemente	*sweetly*
	fácil	fácilmente	*easily*
	feliz	felizmente	*happily, fortunately*

4. When two or more adverbs ending in **-mente** are connected together in the same phrase, all but the last adverb drops the **-mente** suffix:

Example: Mi profesor corrige los exámenes **estricta, severa** y **rigurosamente**
*My teacher corrects the exams strict**ly**, severe**ly** and rigorous**ly***

5. There are many other adverbs which do not follow the rules and you must learn these carefully because they are some of the most commonly used.

	Adverb	**Meaning**	**Adverb**	**Meaning**
Example:	a menudo	*often, frequently*	mal	*badly*
	a propósito	*on purpose, deliberately*	mejor	*better*
	bastante	*enough, sufficiently*	mucho	*much, a lot*
	bien	*well*	peor	*worse*
	de prisa	*quickly, hurriedly*	poco	*not very much, little*
	demasiado	*too much*	pronto	*right away, quickly*
	despacio	*slowly*	siempre	*always*
	en seguida	*at once, immediately*	todavía	*still, yet*

6. In Spanish, an alternative to the **-mente** ending is to create an adverbial phrase using **con** + noun:

Example:

con frecuencia	*frequently*	con cuidado	*carefully*

POSITION OF ADVERBS? (¿DÓNDE PONER LOS ADVERBIOS?)

It is not easy to make hard and fast rules about where to put the adverb in a sentence because so much depends on the emphasis that you wish to make. This relative flexibility is complicated further by the overall rules governing word order in Spanish, which permit a greater variety of possibilities than exists in English. However, there are several guidelines which will help you:

1. Adverbs are normally placed after the word or words to which they are applied. Adverbs usually come immediately after an intransitive verb.
   In other cases, sometimes they immediately follow the verb, but perhaps more frequently they follow the whole verb + object phrase, thereby introducing subtle changes of emphasis:

Example: Ella escribe **constantemente** en su diario
She is constantly writing in her diary (intransitive)

Toca el piano **a menudo**
He plays the piano frequently
(The act of playing the piano is what he does frequently)

Toca **a menudo** el piano, la trompeta y el violín
He frequently plays the piano, the trumpet and the violin
or *Frequently he plays the piano, the trumpet and the violin*
or even *He plays the piano, the trumpet and the violin frequently*
(The act of playing a musical instrument is what he does frequently, be it a piano, a trumpet or a violin)

Ella juega a los naipes y al ajedrez **expertamente**
She plays cards and chess expertly
(She is equally adept at playing **both** cards **and** chess)

Note that, **unlike** English, it is perfectly possible and indeed fairly common to insert the adverb between verb and object. You cannot say "He plays **frequently** the piano", but you can say "Toca **a menudo** el piano".

2. Some adverbs of time and place can precede the verb, especially for emphasis:

Example:	Lo vamos a hacer **ahora**	*We are going to do it now*
	Ahora lo vamos a hacer	*We are going to do it right now*
	Haremos la hoguera **aquí**	*We shall make the bonfire here*
	Aquí (mismo) haremos la hoguera	*We shall make the bonfire (right) here*

3. In Spanish, the auxiliary verb **haber** and the past participle are never separated by an adverb (as the equivalents can be in English):

Example: He viajado en avión **raramente** *I have rarely travelled by plane*
Había estudiado el plan **cuidadosamente**
He had carefully studied the plan (or: *He had studied the plan carefully*)

COMPARISON OF ADVERBS (LA COMPARACIÓN DE LOS ADVERBIOS)

Comparative Adverbs (Los adverbios comparativos)

The **Comparative** is formed by using **más ... que**, **menos ... que**, or **tan ... como** with the adverb:

Example: Mi hermano nada **más** rápidamente **que** mi padre
My brother swims more quickly than my father
Corro **menos** rápidamente **que** mi hijo
I don't run as fast as my son
Mi marido conduce **tan** bien **como** su hermano
My husband drives as well as his brother

Superlative Adverbs (Los adverbios superlativos de superioridad y de inferioridad)

The **Superlative** is identical in appearance to the **Comparative** and the appropriate meaning is understood or inferred from the context:

Example: Aunque sé cinco idiomas, me expreso **más** fácilmente en español
Although I know five languages, I express myself most easily in Spanish
Entre mis amigos, es Pedro quien va **menos** frecuentemente a la piscina
Among my friends, Pedro is the one who goes least often to the swimming pool

Irregular Comparisons

Four Spanish adverbs have irregular comparative forms; they are all very common, so you should learn them carefully:

1. **mucho** *a lot* becomes **más** *more/most*:

Example: Yo hablo **mucho**, mi hermana habla **más**, pero es mi hermano quien **más** habla
I talk a lot, my sister talks more, but it is my brother who talks most (of all)

2. **poco** *little* becomes **menos** *less/least*:

Example: Yo como **poco**, mi prima come aun **menos**, pero es mi tío quien **menos** come
I eat little, my cousin eats even less, but it is my uncle who eats least (of all)

3. **bien** *well* becomes **mejor** *better/best*:

Example: El equipo inglés jugó **bien**, el equipo indio jugó **mejor**,
pero es el equipo australiano el que jugó **mejor** de todos
The English team played well, the Indian team played better,
but the Australian team played best out of all of them

4. **mal** *badly* becomes **peor** *worse/worst*:

Example: Mi amigo canta **mal**, yo canto aun **peor**, pero es mi padre quien **peor** canta
My friend sings badly, I sing worse still, but my father sings worst (of all)

Adverbial Comparisons with a Verb Clause

In Spanish, if the second part of the comparison is a clause that contains a verb but no noun or pronoun serving as the point of comparison, the phrase **de lo que** must be used:

Example: Ella canta **más** dulcemente **que** un ángel
She sings more sweetly than an angel
but: Ella cantó **más** dulcemente **de lo que** se creía posible
She sang more sweetly than was thought possible

MORE ADVERBS (¡MÁS ADVERBIOS!)

Note that when used to form questions, **adónde, cuánto, cómo, cuándo** and **dónde** are written with an accent. See page 7.

adonde	¿**Adónde** vas tan de prisa?	***Where*** *are you off* ***to*** *in such a hurry?*
aun	Esa tarea es **aun** más difícil	*That task is* ***even*** *more difficult*
bastante	El paquete es **bastante** grande Escribe **bastante** despacio	*The packet is* ***quite*** *big* *He writes* ***fairly*** *slowly*
cuanto	¿**Cuánto** vale esta chaqueta? ¿**Cuánto** dura esta ópera? Debes hacerlo **cuanto** antes	***How much*** *does this jacket cost?* ***How long*** *does this opera last?* *You should do it as soon as possible*
como	Tengo **como** veinte sombreros ¿**Cómo** va todo? ¿**Cómo** te llamas? ¿**Cómo**? ¿Qué has dicho? ¡**Cómo**! ¡No lo creo!	*I have* ***something like*** *twenty hats* ***How*** *is everything going?* ***What*** *is your name?* ***Pardon****? What did you say?* ***What****! I don't believe it!*
cuando	¿**Cuándo** te levantas? ¿Es para **cuándo**? El sábado pasado **cuando** estuve en Worcester	***When*** *do you get up?* ***When*** *is it for?* *Last Saturday* ***when*** *I was in Worcester*
donde	La ciudad **donde** vivo ¿De **dónde** eres tú?	*The city* ***where/in which*** *I live* ***Where*** *are <u>you</u> from?*
entonces	Ella vivía en Madrid **entonces**	*She lived in Madrid* ***then/at that time***
luego	Comió y **luego** bebió un café	*He ate and* ***then*** *he drank a coffee*
también	¡Yo quiero ir **también**!	*<u>I</u> want to go* ***too****!*
tanto	No debes gritar **tanto**	*You shouldn't shout* ***so much***
tarde	¡Siempre llego **tarde**!	*I always arrive* ***late****!*
temprano	Los pájaros se despiertan **temprano**	*Birds wake up* ***early***
todavía	El tren no ha llegado **todavía**	*The train has not arrived* ***yet***
ya	¿**Ya** lo sabías tú?	*Did <u>you</u>* ***already*** *know that?*

ARTICLES (LOS ARTÍCULOS)

There are three types of article that you will need to be able to use: definite, indefinite and 'lo'.

THE DEFINITE ARTICLE (EL ARTÍCULO DEFINIDO)

This is the equivalent of the English *the.* Spanish has four forms, **el, la, los, las**.

El is used with singular masculine nouns:

el chico	*the boy*	**el** perro	*the dog*	**el** muro	*the wall*

La is used with singular feminine nouns:

la mujer	*the woman*	**la** mariposa	*the butterfly*	**la** casa	*the house*

El is used directly in front of singular feminine nouns which begin with a stressed vowel "a" or with a silent "h" before stressed vowel "a":

	el agua (*f*)	*the water*	**el** águila (*f*)	*the eagle*	**el** haba (*f*)	*the bean*
but:	**la** agricultura	*agriculture*	**La** Habana	*Havana*	**la** otra arma	*the other weapon*

Los is always used with plural masculine nouns:

los muchachos	*the boys*	**los** peces	*fish*	**los** mapas (*m*)	*the maps*

Las is always used with plural feminine nouns:

las hijas	*the daughters*	**las** ballenas	*the whales*	**las** ciudades	*the cities*

When **el** is used with **a** to mean *to/at the,* the two words are combined as **al**:

Example: Voy **al** almacén (= a + el) — *I'm going to the department store*
Llegaremos **al** puerto mañana (= a + el) — *We'll arrive at the port tomorrow*

No spelling changes are needed for **a + la**, **a + los** or **a + las**.

When **el** is used with **de** to mean *of the*, the two words are combined as **del**:

Example: delante **del** palacio (= de + le) — *in front of the palace*

No spelling changes are needed for **de + la**, **de** + **los** or **de** + **las**.

The definite article is needed in the following situations:

1. With nouns which refer to a particular object or person:
   Example: **El** muchacho está en **el** jardín
   The boy is in the garden

2. With nouns (both abstract and concrete) used in a general sense:
   Example: **La** historia me interesa pero prefiero **la** geografía
   I find history interesting, but I prefer geography
   El café es mi bebida predilecta
   Coffee is my favourite drink
   Me gustan **los** hámsteres pero me encantan **los** conejillos de Indias
   I like hamsters but I love guinea pigs

3. With the names of heaven and hell:
   Example: entre **el** cielo y **el** infierno — *between heaven and hell*

4. When speaking about parts of the body and articles of clothing:

Example:	Ella no se había peinado **el** pelo	*She hadn't combed her hair*
	¿Te has puesto **los** vaqueros?	*Have you put on your jeans?*

5. In phrases using people's titles or ranks or people's names with an adjective:

Example:	**La** Reina Sofía	*Queen Sofia*
	El profesor Hernández	*Professor Hernández*
	La señora López te llamó	*Señora López called you*
	El pobre Juan - ¡está enfermo!	*Poor Juan - he is ill!*

Note that the definite article is dropped in direct address:

Example:	¡Doctor Martín, necesito verle!	*Doctor Martín, I need to see you!*

6. With the names of a few countries and the names of mountains, places, streets and languages:

Example: **La** India es más grande que **El** Salvador
India is bigger than El Salvador
but: España es un país mediterráneo
Spain is a Mediterranean country

Ver **el** Mont Blanc de cerca es emocionante
Seeing Mont Blanc close up is exciting
He visitado **Los** Angeles, **La** Habana, y **El** Cairo
I have visited Los Angeles, Havana and Cairo
La librería en **la** calle de San Mateo
The bookshop on/in St Matthew Street
No es muy difícil aprender **el** castellano
It's not very difficult to learn Castilian
but: Se habla francés
French spoken here (sign in a shop window)

7. In phrases with nouns that have been numbered:

Example:	Puedes tomar **el** barco 5	*You can take boat 5*

8. In phrases concerned with the rate or price of something:

Example:	Lo vendo a cinco euros **el** metro	*I'm selling it at 5 euros per metre*

The definite article is <u>omitted</u> in Spanish where it normally appears in English in just a few instances:

1. In certain idiomatic expressions:

Example:	París, a orillas del Sena	*Paris, on **the** banks of the Seine*
	a instancias de mi esposa	*at **the** request of my wife*

2. Before an unqualified noun in apposition:

Example:	Roma, capital de Italia	*Rome, **the** capital of Italy*
but:	Roma, la hermosa capital de Italia	*Rome, the beautiful capital of Italy*

3. When ordinal numbers qualify proper names:

Example:	Isabel segunda	*Elizabeth **the** Second*

The Indefinite article (El Artículo Indefinido)

In the singular, **un** (*m*) and **una** (*f*) is the equivalent of the English *a, an, any.*
In the plural, **unos** (*m*) and **unas** (*f*) is the equivalent of the English *some, any.*

Example:

Tengo **un** loro que habla y **una** tortuga que no hace ruido alguno
I have a parrot who speaks and a tortoise who doesn't make a sound
Compramos **unos** melocotones y **unas** manzanas para comer en la playa
We bought some peaches and apples to eat on the beach

(In Spanish, if the article is used, it is needed before <u>each</u> noun in a list)

You will notice that there are quite a few occasions on which the article is <u>not</u> needed in Spanish where we would use it in English:

1. When stating a person's job or stating a profession a person took up (with hacerse), if the occupation is not qualified by an adjective:

   Example:

	Se hizo antropóloga	*She became* ***an*** *anthropologist*
	Es profesor	*He is* ***a*** *teacher*
but:	Es **un** profesor excelente	*He's* ***an*** *excellent teacher*

2. In phrases involving **ser, tener, buscar, comprar, llevar** and other similar verbs where the unspecified or generic noun is unqualified:

   Example:

	¿Tienes fuego?	*Have you got* ***a*** *light?* (for a cigarette)
	Siempre lleva sombrero	*He always wears* ***a*** *hat*
	Es soltero	*He's* ***a*** *bachelor*
but:	Es **un** soltero que busca novia	*He's* ***a*** *bachelor looking for* ***a*** *girlfriend*

3. Before numbers such as **cien** or **mil**:

   Example:

Sólo tengo cien euros	*I only have* ***a*** *hundred euros*
Hay mil alumnos en el instituto	*There are* ***a*** *thousand pupils in the school*

4. With certain adjectives such as **cierto**, **medio**, **otro**, **tal**, etc:

   Example:

Vive en cierto barrio cerca de aquí	*He lives in* ***a*** *certain district near here*
Quiero otro helado	*I want another (=* ***an*** *+ other) ice-cream*

5. In certain phrases involving prepositions such as **como**, **por**, **con**, **sin**, etc:

   Example:

   No haremos los ejercicios **como protesta**
   We won't do the exercises as ***a*** *protest*
   Tras todos sus esfuerzos sólo recibió un apretón de manos **por recompensa**
   After all of his efforts he only received a handshake as ***a*** *reward*
   Quiere comprar un piso **con balcón**
   He wants to buy a flat with ***a*** *balcony*
   Lo podremos hacer **sin problema**
   We'll be able to do it without ***a/any*** *problem*

6. In exclamations:
   Example: ¡Qué día tan hermoso! *What **a** beautiful day!*
   ¡Qué susto me diste! *What **a** fright you gave me!*

7. When a noun is in apposition, even if it is qualified:
   Example: Fui a ver al abogado, experto en ese campo
   *I went to see the lawyer, **an** expert in that field*
   Confío en mi amigo, leal compañero en nuestras aventuras
   *I trust my friend, **a** loyal companion in our adventures*

8. In phrases involving negation:
   Example: Se queja de no recibir cartas
   *He complains about not receiving **any** letters*
   No había en su casa ni abrelatas ni sacacorchos
   *There was neither **a** can-opener nor **a** corkscrew in his house*

The Article "Lo" (El Artículo "Lo")

The article "lo" is not actually used with nouns. It is, instead, used in several other ways.

1. **Lo** when combined with an adjective or past participle (always masculine singular) creates an abstract noun based on the meaning or quality of the word:
   Example: **Lo** difícil de la situación es que ...
   The difficult thing about the situation is that ...
   Vas a perder todo **lo** logrado
   You're going to lose all that has been achieved

2. **Lo** when combined with an adjective or adverb, in the phrase **lo** + adjective/adverb + **que**, serves to emphasize or intensify the meaning:
   Example: No sabes **lo** fáciles **que** han resultado los deberes
   You don't know (just) how easy the homework has turned out to be
   No puedes imaginar **lo** agradablemente **que** pasamos el fin de semana
   You can't imagine (just) how pleasantly we spent the weekend

   Note: the adjective agrees with the noun to which it applies but **lo** is invariable.

3. **Lo de** refers, in an unspecified way, to some matter, affair, business, event, etc whose general characteristics are already known about:
   Example: No hemos hablado sobre **lo de** Dolores
   We haven't talked about that thing with Dolores
   Tenemos que resolver **lo del** coche
   We need to settle that business with the car
   No quiero pensar más en **lo del** año pasado
   I don't want to think any more about what happened last year

4. **Lo** is also incorporated into a number of set phrases, such as **a lo mejor** (*probably, likely*), **por lo tanto** (*so, hence, thus*), **a lo lejos** (*in the distance*), **por lo visto** (*seemingly, apparently*), **a lo largo de …** (*through …, throughout …*), **a lo menos/por lo menos** (*at least*).

CONJUNCTIONS (LAS CONJUNCIONES)

Some conjunctions connect sentences, clauses or words (**y, o, pero**) while others only connect clauses (**antes de que, porque**). Some common conjunctions in Spanish are:

a fin de que Esconderé la llave **a fin de que** no puedas* abrir la maleta
I shall hide the key ***so that*** *you cannot open the suitcase*

a menos que No podré terminarlo **a menos que** reciba* tu ayuda
I won't be able to finish it ***unless*** *I receive your help*

antes de que Quiero limpiar la casa **antes de que** vuelvan* mis padres
I want to clean the house ***before*** *my parents return*

así que No pudimos comprar entradas, **así que** no fuimos al concierto
We weren't able to buy tickets, ***so*** *we didn't go to the concert*
Así que ella se despierte*, pondremos la música
As soon as *she wakes up, we'll turn on the music*

aunque Voy de compras esta tarde **aunque** no tengo mucho dinero
I'm going shopping this afternoon ***although*** *I don't have much money*
Le devolveré los libros **aunque** no los necesite*
I shall return the books to him ***even though*** *he doesn't need them*

como Ganaron los rusos, **como** esperaba todo el mundo
The Russians won, ***as*** *everyone expected*
Como ha llovido mucho, no tendré que regar el jardín hoy
As/Because *it has rained a lot, I won't have to water the garden today*

con tal (de) que Podemos seguir jugando, **con tal (de) que** no hagamos* demasiado ruido
We can go on playing, ***so long/as long as*** *we don't make too much noise*

cuando Siempre le veo **cuando** viene a Madrid
I always see him ***when*** *he comes to Madrid*
Cuando encontré el restaurante, mis amigos ya habían cenado
When *I found the restaurant, my friends had already had supper*
Cuando tengas* tiempo debes leer este libro
When *you have time you should read this book*

después (de) que Te daré el helado **después (de) que** comas* todas las zanahorias
I'll give you the ice-cream ***when/after*** *you've eaten all the carrots*

en cuanto **En cuanto** recibí el cheque, me fui al banco
As soon as *I received the cheque, I went to the bank*

*See Verbs: Use of the Present Subjunctive on page 87

hasta que	Seguiré pintando **hasta que** se ponga* el sol *I shall keep on painting **until** the sun sets*
mientras	Llegó mi amigo **mientras** yo trabajaba en el jardín *My friend arrived **just as/while** I was working in the garden* **Mientras** me trates* de esa manera, no seré tu amigo *I won't be your friend **as long as** you treat me like that*
mientras que	A ella le encanta la música clásica, **mientras que** yo prefiero el jazz *She just loves classical music, **whereas** I prefer jazz*
o (u)	Te escribiré **o** te llamaré la semana próxima *I'll write to you **or** I'll phone you next week*

o → **u** before words beginning with **o** or **ho**

	Había diez **u** once niños en el parque *There were ten **or** eleven children in the park*
para que	¿Qué tengo que hacer **para que** me prestes* atención? *What have I got to do **so that** you'll pay attention to me?*
pero	Me encantaría conducir el coche **pero** sólo tengo catorce años *I would just love to drive the car **but** I'm only fourteen*
porque	No pude salir **porque** llovía *I couldn't go out **because** it was raining*
puesto que	**Puesto que** estás aquí, puedes ayudarme ***Since/As** you're here, you can help me*
sin que	Intentaré tomar la pelota **sin que** lo note* él *I shall try to take the ball **without** him noticing*
sino	No comió sólo una pera, **sino** tres *He didn't eat just one pear, **but** three* Me gustan no sólo los helados **sino** también el sorbete y el yogur helado *I like not only ice-creams **but** also sorbet and frozen yoghurt*
sino que	No me avisó de antemano **sino que** vino directamente a la oficina *He didn't let me know in advance **but** came directly to the office*
y (e)	Tengo un coche, una motocicleta **y** dos bicicletas *I have a car, a motorcycle **and** two bicycles*

y → **e** before words beginning with **i** or **hi**

	Voy frecuentemente a las islas de Menorca **e** Ibiza *I frequently go to the islands of Menorca **and** Ibiza*

*See Verbs: Use of the Present Subjunctive on page 87

NOUNS (LOS SUSTANTIVOS)

All nouns in Spanish - including the names for people, animals, plants and inanimate objects - are either:

Masculine (el, un)			or	**Feminine (la, una)**		
el muchacho	un muchacho	*boy*		la muchacha	una muchacha	*girl*
el perro	un perro	*dog*		la gallina	una gallina	*hen*
el árbol	un árbol	*tree*		la rosa	una rosa	*rose*
el lápiz	un lápiz	*pencil*		la iglesia	una iglesia	*church*

In vocabulary lists, words are usually given with their definite article **el** or **la**:
Example: **el** jardín, **la** casa

However, if a feminine noun begins with a stressed "a" or a silent "h" before a stressed "a", the noun takes **el** and so is often shown with (*f*) afterwards to avoid confusion:
Example: **el** alba (*f*), **el** hambre (*f*)

GENDER PROBLEMS (PROBLEMAS CON EL GÉNERO)

The learning of genders is not easy for native speakers of English. There are some rules which can help you with this task, but the only sure way of getting it right is to learn the gender of each noun as you meet the word for the first time.

Learn: **el** muchacho, **la** bicicleta, **el** coche, **la** batalla, **el** mapa, **el** arpa (*f*), **el** hada (*f*), etc.

There are some general guidelines which can make life a bit easier!

1. Names of males are usually masculine and names of females are usually feminine:
Example:

el hombre	*man*	**el** padre	*father*	**el** marido	*husband*	**el** yerno	*son-in-law*
la mujer	*woman*	**la** madre	*mother*	**la** esposa	*wife*	**la** nuera	*daughter-in-law*

2. Some nouns referring to people have masculine and feminine forms according to the gender of the person under discussion:
Example:

el pintor	*artist (man)*	**la** pintora	*artist (woman)*
el profesor	*teacher (man)*	**la** profesora	*teacher (woman)*
un monje	*monk*	**una** monja	*nun*

In Spanish society, as women begin to occupy jobs traditionally held by men, new forms are currently being coined to cope with these changes: people used to talk of **el** or **la** juez, but now a distinct form is emerging: **la** jueza *judge (woman)*.

3. Sometimes the same word may take either **el** or **la** depending on whether it refers to a man or a woman:
Example:

un taxista	*taxi driver (man)*	**una** taxista	*taxi driver (woman)*
un colega	*colleague (man)*	**una** colega	*colleague (woman)*

4. Some words do not change their gender ever; they are always either **el** or **la**, **un** or **una**, no matter whether the person concerned is man or woman:

el personaje	*the character (in a book or film)*	*man or woman*
un bebé	*a baby*	*boy or girl*
una persona	*a person*	*man or woman*
una víctima	*a victim*	*man or woman*
la gente	*people*	*all men, all women or a mixed group*

5. One quite common noun very unusually changes its gender between the singular and the plural: **el** arte (*m*) *art*, **las** artes (*f*) *the arts*. A very few other nouns have doubtful genders or can admit both. One common example is **el/la** mar *sea*; **el** mar is more literal (and more common), while **la** mar is more poetic or literary. There is also some confusion over **la** dote *dowry* which is usually, but not always, feminine.

6. Whatever their sex, animals generally have only one gender, which needs to be learned.

Example:

un elefante *elephant*	**un** ratón *mouse*	**un** pato *duck*	**un** delfín *dolphin*
una girafa *giraffe*	**una** rata *rat*	**una** oca *goose*	**una** marsopa *porpoise*

7. Some familiar domestic and zoo animals do have a modified form for each sex:

Example:

el león *lion* **la** leona *lioness* **el** perro *dog* **la** perra *bitch*

Notice that **el** gallo *cockerel*, **la** gallina *hen* (also *chicken*), **el** toro *bull*, **la** vaca *cow*, **el** carnero *ram*, **la** oveja *ewe* (also *sheep*), have different words for the two sexes and not just different spellings of the same word. The situation is a little different with **el** caballo *horse* and **la** yegua *mare* where caballo is both the word for horse and the usual word for "male horse", but there is also the separate more technical word **el** semental *stallion*.

8. **Masculine nouns include:**

- The seasons (except la primavera)
- The months of the year: un mayo frío *a cold May*
- The days of the week: un lunes nublado *a cloudy Monday*
- Cardinal numbers
- Measurements and weights in the metric system:
  un metro, un kilo, un litro (except una tonelada métrica)
- Colours: el verde *green*, el rosa *pink*
- Points of the compass: el norte, el sur, el este, el oeste
- Most trees: el ciprés *cypress*, el roble *oak*, el pino *pine*, el olivo *olive*
- Most nouns derived from foreign words: el bistec, el champú, el jazz
- Names of mountains, seas, rivers and lakes:
  los Pirineos, el Atlántico, el Duero, el Guadalquivir, el Tajo, el Támesis
- Paintings named by their artist: un Velázquez, un Goya, un Dalí
- Brand names of most means of transport: un BMW, un Boeing
- Names of wines: un Ribera del Duero, un Burdeos, un clarete
- Names of sports clubs and teams: el Real Atlético de Madrid

9. **Some Masculine word endings**

Nouns ending in the following ways are usually masculine:

-e el cruce, el coche, el montaje, el baile, el chisme, el cisne, el canapé, el tanque, el buitre, el juguete
(exceptions: words ending **-ie**, and el hambre (*f*), la fe)

-o el queso
(exceptions: la mano, la dínamo, la foto, la moto, la radio)

-l el canal, el nivel, el perejil, el sol, el cónsul
(exceptions: la cal, la cárcel, la catedral, la col, la miel, la piel, la sal)

-n el galán, el belén, el boletín, el botón, el atún

-r el lugar, el carácter, el visir, el valor, el tahur
(exceptions: la flor, la labor, la mujer)

-t el cabaret, el cenit, el complot

-y el buey, el rey (exceptions: la ley)

10. **Feminine nouns include:**

- Names of letters of the alphabet: una a, una b
- Most tree fruits: la manzana *apple*, la pera *pear*, la naranja *orange*
- Names of islands and the names of countries and regions ending in unstressed **-a**: las (islas) Baleares, las (islas) Canarias, España, Francia, Inglaterra, Alemania, Italia, Suiza, Holanda, Bélgica, Dinamarca, Andorra, Galicia, Navarra, La Mancha
(a few names of countries and regions are masculine: Luxemburgo, (los) Estados Unidos, (el) Canadá, (el) Perú, (el) Japón, Aragón)
- Names of main roads: la M30, la N5
- Names of businesses: la BMW, la Avis

11. **Some Feminine word endings**

Words ending in the following ways are usually feminine:

-a la pierna (there are quite a lot of exceptions: eg (el) Canadá, el día, el gorila, el mapa, el pirata, el planeta, el poeta, el sofá, el tranvía; *plus* many words ending in **-ma**: eg el aroma, el clima, el crucigrama, el diagrama, el dilema, el diploma, el drama, el emblema, el esquema, el fantasma, el panorama, el pijama, el poema, el problema, el programa, el sistema, el telegrama, el tema)

-d la verdad, la lealtad, la pared, la lid, la longitud
(exceptions: el ataúd, el césped, el huésped)

-ie la calvicie, la planicie (exception: el pie)

-ión la organización, la sesión (exceptions: el avión, el camión,)

-itis la apendicitis

-sis la diagnosis, la hipótesis (exceptions: el análisis, el énfasis, el paréntesis)

-umbre la lumbre, la muchedumbre, la pesadumbre

-z la paz, la lucidez, la cicatriz, la coz, la cruz (exceptions: el capataz, el disfraz, el pez, el desliz, el lápiz, el maíz, el matiz, el tapiz, el arroz)

Masculine Nouns and their Feminine Forms (Los Sustantivos Masculinos y sus Formas Femeninas)

As has already been seen, some nouns have entirely different words for the masculine and feminine forms (eg hombre *man,* mujer *woman*; carnero *ram,* oveja *ewe*). However, many nouns in Spanish have very similar masculine and feminine forms.

1. The usual way to make the feminine form of a masculine noun is to change the final **-o** to **-a**, and of course change the article from **el/un** to **la/una:**

Example:	un compañero	una compañera	*companion*
	el primo	la prima	*cousin*

2. Masculine nouns ending in **-a** often show no change in the feminine form:

Example:	un artista	una artista	*artist, artiste*
	el atleta	la atleta	*athlete*

3. Many masculine nouns ending in **-e** also show no change in the feminine form:

Example:	un estudiante	una estudiante	*student*
	un adolescente	una adolescente	*teenager*
but:	el infante	la infanta	*prince/princess*

4. Many other nouns follow the same rules regarding the formation of the feminine form as those which apply to Spanish adjectives. Masculine nouns ending in a consonant normally add an **-a** to create the feminine form:

Example:	un huésped	*guest (m)*	una huéspeda	*guest (f)*
	el colegial	*schoolboy*	la colegiala	*schoolgirl*
	un anfitrión	*host (m)*	una anfitriona	*hostess*
	un burgués	*a member of the middle class (m)*	una burguesa	*a member of the middle class (f)*
but:	un joven	*a young man*	una joven	*a young woman*

Adjectives of nationality also function as nouns: español, española *Spanish,* un español *a Spaniard (m)*, una española *a Spaniard (f)*

5. Some masculine nouns ending in **-e** are changed into the feminine form by adding **-sa**:

Example:	el conde	la condesa	*count/countess*
	el tigre	la tigresa	*tiger/tigress*

6. Some masculine nouns are changed into the feminine form by removing the final vowel and adding **-isa**:

Example:	el poeta	la poetisa	*poet/poetess*
	el sacerdote	la sacerdotisa	*priest/priestess*

7. Some nouns have a less predictable modified form for the feminine:

Example:	el príncipe	*prince*	la princesa	*princess*
	el actor	*actor*	la actriz	*actress*
	el héroe	*hero*	la heroína	*heroine*
	el rey	*king*	la reina	*queen*

Additional information about genders

Some words have two genders and two different meanings. Common examples are:

el capital	*capital (money)*	la capital	*capital (city)*
el caza	*fighter (plane)*	la caza	*hunt, hunting*
el corte	*cut*	la corte	*(royal) court*
el cura	*priest*	la cura	*cure*
el frente	*front (war, weather)*	la frente	*forehead*
el guardia	*police officer*	la guardia	*guard duty*
el guía	*guide (m)*	la guía	*guidebook, guide (f)*
el orden	*order (sequence, neatness)*	la orden	*order (command, religious group)*
el pendiente	*earring*	la pendiente	*slope*
el pez	*fish*	la pez	*pitch (tar)*
el policía	*policeman*	la policía	*police (force)*
el radio	*radius*	la radio	*radio*

Plurals of Nouns (Los Plurales de los Sustantivos)

When you are writing Spanish, it is vital to know whether nouns are masculine or feminine, singular or plural, because their accompanying adjectives must agree in both number and gender and you must also choose the correct verb forms.
It is helpful to remember that many rules concerning the formation of plurals of nouns are very similar or identical to the rules governing the plurals of adjectives.

1. To make nouns plural you change the form of the article and that of the noun itself.

   The definite article 'el' changes to **los** and 'la' changes to **las**:

   los chicos, **los** perros, **los** árboles, **las** muchachas, **las** gallinas, **las** iglesias

   The indefinite article 'un' becomes **unos** and 'una' becomes **unas**:

   unos chicos, **unos** árboles, **unas** muchachas, **unas** vacas, etc

2. Many nouns end in a final unstressed vowel, and so the most usual way of making a noun plural is simply to add **-s** to the singular:
   Example: el gato→los gato**s** *cats* la girafa→las girafa**s** *giraffes*
   el pie→los pie**s** *feet* el juguete→los juguete**s** *toys*

3. Nouns ending with the stressed vowel **-é** and **-ó** also add **-s** to become plural:
   Example: el café→los café**s** *cafés* el buró→los buró**s** *writing desks*
   el té→los té**s** *teas*

   Some irregular plurals are also formed in the same way with stressed **-á** and **-ú**:
   Example: un papá→unos papá**s** *daddies* una mamá→unas mamá**s** *mummies*
   el sofá→los sofá**s** *sofas* el menú→los menú**s** *menus*

4. Nouns ending with the stressed vowel **-á**, **-í** or **-ú** add **-es** to become plural:
   Example: un panamá→unos panamá**es** *panama hats*
   el alhelí→los alhelí**es** *wallflowers*
   el tabú→los tabú**es** *taboos*

5. Nouns which end with consonants generally add **-es** to create the plural:
   Example: la ciudad→las ciudad**es** *cities* el reloj→los reloj**es** *clocks*
   el fusil→los fusil**es** *guns* la ley→las ley**es** *laws*
   la flor→las flor**es** *flowers*

   (i) Nouns with a written accent on the last syllable no longer require it in the plural.
   Example: el gañán→los gañ**anes** *farmhands*
   el autobús→los autob**uses** *buses*

   (ii) Nouns ending in **-n** with no written accent on the last syllable require one on the last syllable but two in the plural form to maintain the correct stress.
   Example: el dictamen→los dict**á**menes *reports*

6. Nouns whose singular ends in **-z** also add **-es**, but the **-z** changes to **-c-** before **-es**:
   Example: el lápiz→los lápi**<u>c</u>es** *pencils* la voz→las vo**<u>c</u>es** *voices*

7. Nouns whose last syllable is <u>not</u> stressed and ends in **-s** are invariable and retain the same form for the plural:
   Example: un paracaídas→unos paracaídas *parachutes*
   el jueves→los jueves *Thursdays*
   el cactus→los cactus *cacti*

8. Spanish nouns deriving from foreign words ending with a consonant just add **-s** to form the plural:
   Example: el pub→los pub**s** *pubs*
   el bistec→los bistec**s** *steaks*
   el carnet→los carnet**s** *ID card, licences*

9. Some nouns only exist in the singular form, as in English:
   Example: el tenis *tennis*

10. Some nouns only exist in the plural form:
   Example: las afueras *outskirts* las tinieblas *shadows, darkness*
   las tijeras *scissors* los auriculares *headphones*

   and some have a singular form but are much more commonly used in the plural:
   Example: las vacaciones *holidays* los pantalones *trousers*

11. Some nouns have different meanings according to whether they are in the singular or the plural:
   Example: el entremés *interlude* los entremeses *hors d'œuvres*
   una escalera *staircase, ladder* las escaleras *stairs*
   el fondo *bottom, depth* los fondos *funds*
   la gafa *hook, clamp* las gafas *glasses, spectacles*
   la gracia *grace, humour* las gracias *thanks*
   la seña *sign* las señas *details, address*

12. When talking about several members of a single family by their surname, Spanish does not make a plural of the surname, as does English:

    Example: the Hendersons **but**: los García

    but when referring to all people sharing the same surname, a plural is formed when and if possible:

    Example: todos los Monteros en la guía telefónica
    all the people called Montero in the telephone directory

DIMINUTIVE AND AUGMENTATIVE SUFFIXES (SUFIJOS DIMINUTIVOS Y AUMENTATIVOS)

Spanish has a wide range of suffixes which can be attached to the end of nouns. The most frequently occurring suffixes are those which make the noun smaller (diminutive) or bigger (augmentative). Compare the English suffix *-let*: play→playlet (*a short play*).

The commonest diminutive suffixes in Spanish are **-ito, -ita, -itos, -itas** and **-illo, -illa, -illos, -illas**, and the commonest augumentatives are **-ón, ona, -ones, -onas**.

Example: Todo lo que hay que saber está en este lib**rito**
Everything you need to know is in this little/short book
Podrás ver mejor con esta lampar**illa**
You'll be able to see better with this little lamp
Comiendo mucho, se convirtió en un hombr**ón**
By eating a lot he turned into a hulky man

COMPOUND NOUNS (SUSTANTIVOS COMPUESTOS)

This is the name given to nouns which are made up from two elements, usually either **verb + noun** or **noun + noun**. When you meet compound nouns, the best way is to learn each one with its plural because there are various patterns for forming compound nouns, and the plurals can vary according to how the compound noun is made up. Many compound nouns in Spanish end with an unstressed **-as** or **-os**, and in those cases there is no change in the plural.

Example: **el parabrisas** *windscreen* → **los parabrisas** *windscreens*
this is a verb + noun (literally "stop-breezes") and as it ends in unstressed **-as** it is invariable, not changing at all in the plural

el hombre rana *frogman* → **los hombres rana** *frogmen*
this is a noun + noun compound with only one change, as in English: we don't say *frogsmen*

Here are some other common compound nouns:

el/los lavavajillas	*dishwasher/s* (literally "wash-crockeries")
el/los parachoques	*shock-absorber/s* (literally "stop-shocks")
el/los abrelatas	*can-opener/s* (literally "open-tins")
el/los tocadiscos	*record-player/s* (literally "play-disks")
el/los rascacielos	*skyscraper/s* (literally "scratch-skies")
el aire acondicionado	*air conditioning* (conceptually has no plural)
la/las fecha(s) tope	*deadline/s* (literally "date-limit")
la/las ciudad(es) jardín	*garden city/cities*

Almost all verb + noun compound nouns in Spanish are masculine in gender; noun + noun compounds follow the gender of the "base" noun.

COLLECTIVE NOUNS (SUSTANTIVOS COLECTIVOS)

Some nouns are singular in form although they are plural in meaning and they therefore take a **singular** verb in Spanish.
Some common ones are: la gente *people*, la familia *family*, la mayoría *majority*, la minoría *minority*, la policía *police*, la muchedumbre *crowd* and la tripulación *crew*:

Example:	La gente **quiere** precios bajos	*People want low prices*
	La familia **está** en casa	*The family is at home*
	La mayoría **pide** elecciones	*The majority is asking for elections*
	La muchedumbre **esperaba**	*The crowd was waiting*

El ganado *livestock* is a common collective noun for animals: **el ganado mayor** refers to *cattle, horses and mules*, while **el ganado menor** refers to *sheep, pigs and goats*.

THE POSSESSIVE CASE (EL POSESIVO)

To show ownership there is no equivalent of the apostrophe **s** which we have in English. Instead, with proper names, you have to use the word **de**:

Example:	el sombrero **de** Juan	*Juan's hat*
	la falda **de** Ana	*Ana's skirt*

With other nouns you use **de** + the article + the noun.
This means that you have to be careful with masculine and plural nouns:

Example:	el perro **del** muchacho	*the boy's dog* (1 dog,1 boy)
	el perro **de la** muchacha	*the girl's dog* (1 dog, 1 girl)
	el perro **del** niño	*the child's dog* (1 dog, 1 child)
	el perro **de los** niños	*the children's dog* (1 dog, more than 1 child)
	el perro **de los** muchachos	*the boys' dog* (1 dog, more than 1 boy)
	el perro **de las** muchachas	*the girls' dog* (1 dog, more than 1 girl)

NUMBERS, MEASUREMENTS, TIME AND DATES (LOS NÚMEROS, LAS MEDIDAS, LA HORA Y LA FECHA)

CARDINAL NUMBERS (NÚMEROS CARDINALES)

0	cero	20	veinte	100	ciento (cien)
1	uno (un), una	21	veintiuno (-ún), -una	101	ciento uno
2	dos	22	veintidós	199	ciento noventa y nueve
3	tres	23	veintitrés	200	doscientos, -as
4	cuatro	24	veinticuatro	201	doscientos uno
5	cinco	25	veinticinco	250	doscientos cincuenta
6	seis	26	veintiséis	300	trescientos, -as
7	siete	27	veintisiete	400	cuatrocientos, -as
8	ocho	28	veintiocho	500	quinientos, -as
9	nueve	29	veintinueve	600	seiscientos, -as
10	diez	30	treinta	700	setecientos, -as
11	once	31	treinta y uno (un), una	800	ochocientos, -as
12	doce	32	treinta y dos	900	novecientos, -as
13	trece	33	treinta y tres	1000	mil
14	catorce	40	cuarenta	1001	mil uno
15	quince	50	cincuenta	1909	mil novecientos nueve
16	dieciséis	60	sesenta	1981	mil novecientos ochenta y uno
17	diecisiete	70	setenta	1999	mil novecientos noventa y nueve
18	dieciocho	80	ochenta	2012	dos mil doce
19	diecinueve	90	noventa	100.000	cien mil
		99	noventa y nueve	1.000.000	un millón
				10.000.000	diez millones

You should learn the following points:

1. In writing all figures over one thousand, a full stop is normally used, while a comma indicates a decimal point: 500.000 *five hundred thousand*; 15,25 *fifteen point two five*; this does **not** apply to dates, which are normally written without punctuation.

2. **Uno** shortens to **un** immediately before a masculine singular noun: **un** ojo *an/one eye*, and agrees with a feminine singular noun: una niña *a/one girl*; **una** shortens to **un** before a stressed **a** or **ha**: **un** ala (*f*) *a/one wing*, **un** haba (*f*) *a/one bean.*

3. Higher numbers ending in -**uno** combined with plural nouns agree in gender with the noun: veintiún soldados *twenty-one soldiers*, noventa y una botellas *ninety-one bottles*, cincuenta y un mil coches *fifty-one thousand cars*, veintiuna mil flores *twenty-one thousand flowers.*

4. 16 to 19 and 21 to 29 are normally written as **one** word (writing them as three is old-fashioned); 31-39 through to 91-99, however, are normally written as **three** words.

5. The elements within larger numbers are not connected by **y**, except where y is already part of an element; thus 400.115 cuatrocientos mil | ciento quince, but 8.765.432 ocho millones | setecientos *sesenta* **y** *cinco* mil | cuatrocientos *treinta* **y** *dos.*

6. **Ciento** alone means **one** hundred; **ciento** shortens to **cien** when it comes immediately before masculine and feminine nouns and adjectives: cien caballos *a hundred horses, **one** hundred horses*, cien buenas películas *a/**one** hundred good films.* **Ciento** also takes the shortened form **cien** when it comes before another numeral that it is multiplying, eg cien mil, cien millones, but **not** in other compound numerals, eg ciento cincuenta pájaros *one hundred and fifty birds.*

7. **Doscientos** to **novecientos** agree in gender when used with a noun: trescientas casas *300 houses*, quinientos cincuenta y un libros *551 books*, la página doscientas quince *page 215.*

8. **Mil** alone means **one** thousand, and is only preceded by **un** when itself being multiplied by a numeral that ends in **un**: 31.000 treinta y un mil, 301.000 trescientos un mil. 1001, 1002 are written mil uno, mil dos, etc, but before a noun the conjunction **y** is added: las mil **y** una noches *the thousand and one nights.*

9. The alternative English forms, eg eleven hundred instead of one thousand one hundred, do **not** have an equivalent in Spanish; this also applies to dates.

10. Unlike ciento and mil, **un millón is** preceded by the indefinite article; note also that, unlike English, it has a plural form, dos millon**es**, tres millon**es,** and that it is linked to nouns with de: cinco millon**es de** euros *five million euros.*

11. "Odd" after a numeral is rendered as **tantos**:
    Necesitamos cincuenta y **tantos** cuchillos *We need fifty-odd knives.*

12. All numbers are masculine: ¿Es **un** cinco o **un** nueve? *Is it a five or a nine?*

13. Percentages (los porcentajes) are expressed using por: diez por ciento *10%*, ciento por ciento *100%*; unlike English, the article is used is most phrases: **el** noventa por ciento de los estudiantes aprobaron el examen 90% *of the students passed the exam*, la inflación ha subido **un** cinco por ciento *inflation has risen by 5%.*

14. Fractions/las fracciones (mathematical):

$^1/_2$ un medio	$^1/_4$ un cuarto	$^1/_3$ un tercio
$1^1/_2$ uno y medio	$^3/_4$ tres cuartos	$^2/_3$ dos tercios

In other contexts parts of a whole are expressed in a variety of different ways:

medio, -a is an adjective:

medio kilo de harina *half a kilo of flour*
media botella de vino *half a bottle of wine*

medio can also function as an (invariable) adverb:

Ella llegó **medio** helada *She arrived half frozen*

In many expressions half is rendered by **la mitad de**:

la mitad del mundo **or** medio mundo *half the world*
Dame **la mitad de** tu bocadillo *Give me half of your sandwich*
la primera mitad del partido de fútbol *the first half of the football match*

Other fractions combine the ordinal numeral with **la parte de**:

la tercera **parte del** ejército *a third of the army*
las tres cuartas **partes del** público *three quarters of the audience*

15. Telephone numbers are read out in groups of two or three:
example: 91-555-1234 would be read as:
noventa y uno | cinco, cincuenta y cinco | doce, treinta y cuatro

ORDINAL NUMBERS (NÚMEROS ORDINALES)

In English, these are the words *first, second, third, fourth* etc.
In Spanish, as in English, the most commonly used ordinals are the lowest numbers:

1st	primero (primer)	6th	sexto
2nd	segundo	7th	séptimo
3rd	tercero	8th	octavo
4th	cuarto	9th	noveno
5th	quinto	10th	décimo

There are also distinct forms in Spanish for the tens, hundreds, thousands, millions and beyond; the teens are covered by compounds based on *décimo*, and thereafter a sure sign of an ordinal is the suffix *-ésimo*. The higher the ordinal, the less likely it is to be used in normal speech or writing. Usually higher ordinals are replaced by cardinals: en su cuarenta aniversario de bodas *on their fortieth wedding anniversary*, Alfonso trece *Alfonso XIII/Alfonso the thirteenth*, el siglo veinte *the twentieth century*.

Ordinals function as normal adjectives, agreeing in number and gender, and usually preceding the noun: **la** tercer**a** vez *the third time,* **los** octav**os** Juegos Olímpicos *the 8th Olympic Games*, but note Carlos quint**o** *Charles V*, Isabel segund**a** *Elizabeth II.*

Notice that, like a number of other common adjectives, **primero** and **tercero** shorten to **primer** and **tercer** when directly before a masculine singular noun: el **primer** ruido que oí *the first sound I heard*, el **tercer** edificio a la izquierda *the third building on the left,* but **not** when separated by an adjective: el **tercero** y más distante planeta *the third and most distant planet.*

The abbreviations 1st, 2nd, 3rd, etc are: 1º (1er)/1ª, 2º/2ª, 3º (3er)/3ª, etc

DISTANCE AND DIMENSIONS (LA DISTANCIA Y LAS DIMENSIONES)

¿Cuánto hay de aquí a Barcelona?	*How far is it to Barcelona?*
¿Está cerca? ¿Está lejos?	*Is it near? Is it far?*
¿Queda cerca? ¿Queda lejos?	*Is it near? Is it far?*
La tienda está a sólo unos metros de mi casa	*The shop is just a few metres from my house*
El castillo está a cinco kilómetros	*It's five kilometres to the castle (The castle is five kilometres away)*
El hotel está cerca de la playa	*The hotel is near the beach*
¿Cuánto tiene esa caja de largo/alto/ancho?	*How long/high/wide is that box?*
La moda determina el largo de los abrigos	*Fashion determines the length of coats*
El barco tiene cien metros de largo	*The boat is a hundred metres long*
El edificio tiene treinta metros de alto	*The building is thirty metres high*
La calle tiene diez metros de ancho	*The street is ten metres wide*
El lago tiene tres metros de hondo	*The lake is three metres deep*

TELLING THE TIME (LA HORA)

¿Qué hora es?	*What time is it?*
¿Tiene(s) la hora?	*Can you tell me the time?*
	Do you have the time? (American)
¿Qué hora tienes?	*What time do you make it?*
Es la una	*It is one o'clock*
Son las dos	*It is two o'clock*
Son las tres y cinco	*It is 5 past 3*
Son las cuatro y diez	*It is 10 past 4*
Son las cinco y cuarto	*It is quarter past 5*
Son las seis y veinte	*It is 20 past 6*
Son las siete y veinticinco	*It is 25 past 7*
Son las ocho y media	*It is half past 8*
Son las nueve menos veinticinco	*It is 25 to 9*
Son las diez menos veinte	*It is 20 to 10*
Son las once menos cuarto	*It is quarter to 11*
Es la una menos diez	*It is 10 to 1*
Son las dos menos cinco	*It is 5 to 2*
Son las nueve de la mañana	*It is 9 in the morning*
Son las tres de la tarde	*It is 3 in the afternoon*
Son las once de la noche	*It is 11 at night*
Son las cuatro de la madrugada	*It is 4 at night/in the early morning*
Son las doce	*It is 12 o'clock*
Son las doce y media de la noche	*It is half past midnight*
Es mediodía/Es medianoche	*It is midday/It is midnight*
(mediodía and medianoche cannot be combined with minutes after or to the hour)	
a las veinte horas	*at 20:00*
a las veinte quince	at *20:15*
a las veinte treinta	at *20:30*
Son las cinco en punto	*It is precisely 5 o'clock*
a eso de/alrededor de las seis	*about 6/round about 6*
¿A qué hora vas a llegar?	*When are you going to arrive?*
Tengo una cita a las dos y media	*I have an appointment at 2:30*
Dio la una	*It struck one*
Están dando las diez	*It is just striking ten*
2 horas, 11 minutos y 30 segundos	*2 hours, 11 minutes and 30 seconds*

Parts of the day

Compared to the British day (morning, afternoon, evening, night) the Spanish day is split up rather differently. The period covered by morning - *mañana* is broadly equivalent (from around 5 am to midday). *Mediodía* means 12 noon but can also refer more vaguely to the middle-of-the-day break or lunch time - which in Spain is usually much later than 12 noon. The Spanish word *tarde* covers both afternoon and a good part of the evening (from midday to around 8 pm). Night - *noche* covers a shorter period in Spanish (around 9 pm to around 2 am). Spanish uses a fourth term, *madrugada*, meaning something like "the small hours" or "the pre-dawn hours", to refer to the period from around 2 in the morning to 5 in the morning.

DAYS OF THE WEEK (LOS DÍAS DE LA SEMANA)

lunes	martes	miércoles	jueves	viernes	sábado	domingo
Monday	*Tuesday*	*Wednesday*	*Thursday*	*Friday*	*Saturday*	*Sunday*

Please remember:

- capital letters are not used with days of the week or months of the year, except festivals
- all the days of the week are masculine nouns

Example: El martes tuve un examen	*On Tuesday I had an examination*
Iré al museo el domingo próximo	*I'll go to the museum next Sunday*
La vi el jueves pasado	*I saw her last Thursday*
Suelo ir al cine los viernes	*I usually go to the cinema on Fridays*

(The English **on** is understood but not expressed in Spanish.)

MONTHS OF THE YEAR (LOS MESES DEL AÑO)

enero	febrero	marzo	abril	mayo	junio
January	*February*	*March*	*April*	*May*	*June*
julio	agosto	septiembre	octubre	noviembre	diciembre
July	*August*	*September*	*October*	*November*	*December*

Again, please remember:

- no capital letters are used with days of the week or months of the year
- all the names of the months are masculine nouns; they are often used with the phrase **el mes de/los meses de**:

Example: Siempre paso **los meses de julio y agosto** en Santander
I always spend the months of July and August in Santander

DATES (LA FECHA)

When writing/saying the date in Spanish, you use cardinal numbers for all dates except the first of the month which has the ordinal: **primero**

-¿A cuánto estamos?	*What's the date?*
-Estamos a seis/veinte	*It's the 6th/20th*
-¿Qué fecha es hoy?	*What's today's date?*
-Hoy es el **primero** de septiembre	*Today's the 1st September*
el tres de marzo	*3rd March*
el once de abril	*11th April*
-¿Qué día es hoy?	*What day is it today?*
-Hoy es lunes	*Today's Monday*
-Estamos a sábado	*Today's Saturday*
-¿Cuándo es tu cumpleaños?	*When's your birthday?*
-Mi cumpleaños es el quince de noviembre	*My birthday is 15th November*
el veintiuno de enero	*21st January*
el treinta y uno de agosto	*31st August*

El nació en dos mil tres	*He was born in 2003*
Ella nació el dos **de** mayo **de** mil novecientos noventa	*She was born on 2 May 1990*
El domingo, veinte de agosto	*Sunday, August 20th*
Julio César (100-44 a.C./a. de J.C.)	*Julius Caesar (100-44 BC)*
la invasión de 711 d.C./d. de J.C.	*the invasion of 711 AD*
Granada en/durante los años setenta	*Granada in the 70s/1970s*
en el curso del siglo veinte/XX	*in the course of the 20th century*

Special days of the year (Los días festivos):

la Nochevieja	*New Year's Eve*	el Corpus Christi	*Corpus Christi*
el día de Año Nuevo	*New Year's Day*	el día de Todos los Santos	*All Saints' Day*
el día de Reyes	*Epiphany (Jan 6)*	el día de Difuntos	*All Souls' Day*
el martes de Carnaval	*Shrove Tuesday*	la Nochebuena	*Christmas Eve*
el miércoles de Ceniza	*Ash Wednesday*	el día de Navidad	*Christmas Day*
la Cuaresma	*Lent*	la Pascua	*Passover*
el Domingo de Ramos	*Palm Sunday*	el Año Nuevo judío	*Rosh Hashanah*
el Viernes Santo	*Good Friday*	el día del Perdón	*Yom Kippur*
el Domingo de Pascua	*Easter Sunday*	el Januká	*Hanukkah*
el Domingo de Pentecostés	*Whit Sunday*	el Ramadán	*Ramadan*

Note these idioms:

- **in** Me levanto a las siete **de** la mañana
  I get up at 7 ***in*** *the morning*
  Vuelvo a casa a las seis **de** la tarde
  I come home at 6 o'clock ***in*** *the evening*
  a las ocho **de** la mañana
  at 8 am/at 8 o'clock ***in*** *the morning*
  a las dos **de** la tarde
  at 2 pm/at 2 o'clock ***in*** *the afternoon*

  BUT **Por** la mañana, suelo dar un paseo
  In *the morning, I usually go for a stroll*
  Salimos **dentro de** una hora
  We are leaving ***in*** *an hour*
  Ella leyó el libro **en** tres horas
  She read the book ***in*** *three hours*

- **for** Me quedé allí tres semanas/Me quedé **durante** tres semanas
  I stayed there ***for*** *3 weeks*
  Ella estará en Madrid sólo **por** tres días
  She will be in Madrid ***for*** *only three days*
  Ella lleva un año viviendo en Bilbao
  or Ella vive en Bilbao **desde hace** un año
  She has been living in Bilbao ***for*** *a year*
  (See Special Constructions using the Present Tense on page 73)

- **ago** **hace** tres días — *three days* ***ago***
  hace mucho (tiempo) — *a long time* ***ago***

PREPOSITIONS (LAS PREPOSICIONES)

Here are some of the most widely used Spanish prepositions:

a	Ella va **a** Madrid	*She is going **to** Madrid*
	Dejó caer el vaso **al** suelo	*He dropped the glass **on** the floor* (= *The glass dropped **to** the floor*)
	Daré el libro **a** José	*I shall give the book **to** José*
	¿**A** quién pertenece esto?	*Whose is this? (**To** whom does this belong?)*
	¡Me pertenece **a** mí!	*It's mine! (It belongs **to** me)*
	Lancé la pelota **a** María	*I threw the ball **at (to)** María*
	Los vendo **a** seis euros el kilo	*I'm selling them **at** 6 euros a kilo*
	a las cinco de la tarde	***at** five o'clock in the afternoon*
	al principio de la película	***at** the beginning of the film*
	Jaime quitó el juguete **a** Andrés	*Jaime took the toy (away) **from** Andrés*
	Granada está **a** cien kilómetros	*Granada is a hundred kilometres away* (= *Granada is 100 kms **from** here*)
	la ventana da **al** parque	*the window looks **on to** the park*
	a la derecha/**a** la izquierda	***on** the right/**on** the left*
	a pie/**a** caballo	***on** foot/**on** horseback*
	a propósito	***on** purpose*
	a tientas	***by** touch* (= *groping one's way along*)
	al encender la luz ...	***upon** turning on the light ...*
	me sentaré **al** sol	*I'll sit down **in** the sun*
	de la mañana **a** medianoche	*from morning **till** midnight*

a "personal"

The so-called personal "a" is required after the verb and before the direct object when the direct object is a person, a domestic animal, or something that is being personified:

Roberto quiere **a** Ana	*Roberto loves Ana*
Vislumbré **a** alguien en el jardín	*I glimpsed someone in the garden*
Conchita mima **a** su perro	*Conchita pampers/spoils her dog*
Siempre saludo **a** mis plantas	*I always say hello to my plants*

Exceptions: When the object-noun refers to a **category** of person rather than to a **specific** person etc, personal "a" is <u>not</u> used. Also, the verb **tener** does <u>not</u> take the personal "a":

	Buscan una au pair	*They're looking for an au pair*
BUT	Contrató a un criado llamado Luis	*He hired a servant called Luis*
	Tienen dos gatos simpáticos	*They have two friendly cats*
	Sólo tengo un tío	*I only have one uncle*

acerca de

un libro **acerca de** la historia inglesa	*a book **about** English history*
Me habló **acerca de** su problema	*He talked to me **concerning** his problem*

alrededor (de)

Miraba a su **alrededor**	*He was looking **(around) about** him*
El niño corría **alrededor del** cuarto	*The child was running **around** the room*
una valla **alrededor de** la casa	*a fence **round** the house*

ante

Ante tal situación ...	*When **confronted by** such a situation ...*
No sabía qué hacer **ante** su actitud	*I didn't know what to do **in the face of** his attitude*

antes de

antes de mediodía	***before** midday*
antes de la vuelta de su padre	***before** his father came/comes home*
Antes de marcharse, él ...	***Before** leaving, he ...*
antes de todo	***above** all*
en 100 **antes de** Jesucristo	*in 100 **BC***

aparte de

¿Qué queda **aparte de** esta silla?	*What's left **apart from** this chair?*
Aparte de eso, todo funciona bien	***Besides/Apart from** that, all is going well*

a través de

a través de los campos/siglos	***across/through** the fields/centuries*
entró **a través de** la ventana abierta	*it came in **through** the open window*

bajo

bajo una dictadura	***under** a dictatorship*
se escondió **bajo** las escaleras	*he hid **under/below/beneath** the stairs*
Jugaron al golf **bajo** la lluvia	*They played golf **in** the rain*
dos grados **bajo** lo normal	*two degrees **below** normal*

cerca de

¿Hay un banco **cerca de** aquí?	*Is there a bank **nearby (near** here)?*
El edificio está **cerca de** la carretera	*The building is **near** the road*
Cerca de 50 alumnos partieron ayer	***Almost/Nearly** 50 pupils left yesterday*

con

un teniente **con** dos soldados	*a lieutenant **with** two soldiers*
Ella viene **con**migo	*She comes/is coming **with** me*
una riña **con** su padre	*a quarrel **with** his father*
Es muy severo **con** los alumnos	*He's very severe **with/towards** the pupils*
Ella es generosa **con** su dinero	*She is generous **with** her money*
Lo cortó **con** sus tijeras	*He cut it **with** his scissors*
Pagaré **con** tarjeta de crédito	*I'll pay **by** credit card*
una mujer **con** ojos azules	*a woman **with** blue eyes*
Soñé **con** dragones anoche	*I dreamt **about** dragons last night*
Con lo difícil que es ...	***Given** how difficult it is ...*
con todo	***considering** everything/all the same*

contra

el equipo español **contra** el francés	*the Spanish team **against** the French one*
la pala apoyada **contra** la cerca	*the spade propped **against** the fence*

de

una taza **de** té	*a cup **of** tea*
una camisa **de** algodón	*a cotton shirt*
el coche **de** Rosa	*Rosa**'s** car*
una novela **de** Galdós	*a novel **by** Galdós*
en el mes **de** diciembre	*in (the month **of**) December*
las vacaciones **de** verano	*the summer holidays*
en la sala **de** estar	*in the living room*
Tomó los libros **del** cajón	*He took the books **out of** the drawer*
El zorro salió **del** bosque	*The fox came **out of** the wood*
Vino **de** Sevilla para participar	*He came **from** Seville in order to participate*
¿**De** dónde eres? Soy **de** Londres	*Where are you **from**? I'm **from** London*
de cuatro a ocho	***from** four to eight (o'clock)*
aquella mujer **del** vestido rojo	*that woman over there **in** the red dress*
el tren más rápido **del** mundo	*the fastest train **in** the world*
La tierra está cubierta **de** nieve	*The ground is covered **with** snow*
La mochila está llena **de** libros	*The rucksack is full **of** books*
Este calcetín está lleno **de** agujeros	*This sock is full **of** holes*
Se puso rojo **de** vergüenza	*He turned red **with** embarrassment*
Hay que hacerlo **de** esta manera	*You must do it **(in)** this way*
¿Qué piensas **de** esta solución?	*What do you think **of** this solution?*
más **de** tres millones **de** habitantes	*more **than** 3 000 000 inhabitants*
de día, **de** noche	***by** day, **by** night*
¿Te han contado algo **de** ella?	*Have they told you anything **about** her?*
el monumento más famoso **de** Lugo	*the most famous monument **in** Lugo*
el chico menos paciente **del** mundo	*the least patient boy **in** the world*

(por) debajo de

El zapato está **debajo de** la cama	*The shoe is **under** the bed* (stationary)
El tren corre **por debajo de** la ciudad	*The train runs **underneath** the city* (motion)

(por) delante de

Ella está **delante de** la casa	*She is **in front of** the house* (stationary)
¿Nos veremos **delante del** cine?	*Shall we meet **outside** the cinema?*
Los camiones pasan **por delante de** la fábrica	*The lorries pass by **in front of** the factory* (motion)

dentro de

los soldados **dentro del** castillo	*the soldiers **inside** the castle*
Terminaremos **dentro de** una hora	*We shall finish **in/within** one hour*

desde

desde ayer	***since** yesterday*
desde enero **hasta** marzo	***from** January **(up) to** March*
Mandaron cartas **desde** España	*They sent letters **from** Spain*
desde aquí **hasta** la colina	***from** here **to** the hill*

desde hormigas **hasta** elefantes	***from** ants **to** elephants*
¿**Desde cuándo** estás esperando allí?	***How long** have you been waiting there?*
Vivo en Gijón **desde hace** dos años	*I've been living in Gijón **for** two years*

(see Special Constructions using the present tense on page 73)

después de

después de la representación	***after** the performance*
Después de llegar, ella ...	***After** she arrived, she ...*
después de todo	***after** all/in the long run*
en 100 **después de** Jesucristo	*in 100 **AD***

(por) detrás de

el rostro **detrás de** la máscara	*the face **behind** the mask*
El camino pasa **por detrás del** establo	*The path runs **behind** the stable*

durante

Leyó un libro **durante** la reunión	*He read a book **during** the meeting*
durante mucho tiempo	***for** a long time*

en

Estoy **en** España	*I am **in** Spain*
en la piscina	***in/at** the swimming pool*
en la universidad	***at** university*
en otoño	***in** autumn*
en el año 2014	***in** 2014*
en ese instante	***at** that instant*
en mi caso	***in** my case*
en mi opinión	***in** my opinion*
en voz baja	***in** a low voice*
en catalán	***in** Catalan*
en broma/**en** serio	***as** a joke/**in** earnest, seriously*
Ella se especializa **en** la informática	*She specializes **in** computer science*
Su carácter se revela **en** sus gestos	*His character is revealed **in/by** his gestures*
de aquí **en** una semana	***in** a week's time from now*
Puso la culebra **en** el saco	*He put the snake **in(to)** the bag*
Ella entra **en** la cueva	*She goes/is going **into** the cave*
en la mesa, **en** el suelo	***on/at** the table, **on** the floor*
En mi llegada ...	*When I arrive(d), .../**on** my arrival ...*
Viene **en** coche	*He is coming **by** car*
de vez **en** cuando	*from time **to** time*
Pienso **en** ti	*I'm thinking **about** you*

en cuanto a

En cuanto a mí, me quedo aquí	***As for** me, I'm staying here*
En cuanto a la situación política ...	***As regards** the political situation ...*

(por) encima de

El despacho está **encima del** cine	*The office is **over/above** the cinema*
el pájaro **encima de** la torre	*the bird **on top of** the tower*
Saltó **por encima del** seto	*He jumped **over** the hedge* (motion)

enfrente de

la tienda **enfrente del** ayuntamiento	*the shop **opposite/facing** the town hall*

entre

El diccionario está **entre** la enciclopedia y el almanaque	*The dictionary is **between** the encyclopaedia and the almanac*
entre nosotros	***between** ourselves, just **between** us*
La tienda se abre **entre** las 9 y la 1	*The shop is open **between** 9 and 1*
Estás **entre** amigos	*You are **among** friends*
Hablaban **entre** sí	*They were talking **among** themselves*
Andaba **entre** los árboles	*He was walking **among** the trees*
Entre las zarzas y las ortigas, no pude seguir por el sendero	***What with** the brambles and the nettles, I couldn't continue along the path*

a eso de

a eso de cinco millas/las ocho	***about/around** five miles/eight o'clock*

fuera de

Jugaban **fuera de** la casa	*They were playing **outside** the house*
un sitio **fuera de** la ciudad	*a place **outside (of)** the city*
fuera de peligro	***out of** danger*
Está **fuera de** sí	*He is **beside** himself*

hacia

Ella se dirigía **hacia** la estación	*She was heading **towards** the station*
hacia el norte	***towards/facing** the north*
Ella se volvió **hacia** mí	*She turned **towards** me*
La locomotora iba **hacia adelante**	*The locomotive was going **forwards***
hacia el fin de la semana	***towards** the end of the week*
Vendrá **hacia** las 9	*He'll come **around/about** 9 o'clock*
tu amabilidad **hacia** los extranjeros	*your kindness **towards** foreigners*

hasta

Llegué **hasta** los semáforos	*I got **as far as** the traffic lights*
hasta el pie de la montaña	***as far as/up to** the foot of the mountain*
Había **hasta** dos mil personas allí	*There were **up to** two thousand people there*
hasta medianoche	***up to** midnight/**until** midnight*
desde el principio **hasta** el fin	***from** the beginning **(right) up to** the end*
Es fácil; **hasta** mi hermano sabe eso	*It's easy; **even** my brother knows that*

al lado de

el garaje **al lado de** la casa	*the garage **beside/at the side of** the house*

a lo largo de

Trabajé **a lo largo de** la primavera	*I worked **throughout/all through** the spring*
Había flores **a lo largo del** sendero	*There were flowers **(all) along** the track*

lejos de

un país **lejos de** aquí	*a country **far from** here*

más allá de

el país **más allá de** los Pirineos	*the country **beyond/on the far side of** the Pyrenees*

para

Esto es **para** ti	*This is **for** you*
las tareas **para** la semana entrante	*the tasks **for** next week*
una taza **para** el té	*a teacup (=a cup **for** tea,* **not** *a cup **of** tea)*
Salgo **para** Bruselas esta tarde	*I leave **for** Brussels this afternoon*
¿**Para** cuánto tiempo estás aquí?	*How long are you here **for**?*
Alquilaré un coche **para** mañana	*I shall hire a car **for** tomorrow*
Para ellos el partido era emocionante	*The match seemed exciting **to** them*
El coche tiene muy buena pinta **para** su edad	*The car looks very good **for/considering** its age*
Tengo bastante tiempo **para** hacerlo	*I have enough time **to** do it*
Vendo flores **para** ganar dinero	*I sell flowers **(in order) to** earn money*
Llegaré **para** las seis	*I'll arrive **by** six*

para con

Es amable **para con** sus parientes	*He's kind/nice **to** his relatives*
tu actitud **para con** tus amigos	*your attitude **towards** your friends*

a partir de

A partir de hoy llegaré a las ocho	***Starting from** today, I'll arrive at eight*
El museo está abierto **a partir de** las diez	*The museum is open **from** ten o'clock **onwards***

a pesar de

Iremos **a pesar de** su oposición	*We shall go **in spite of** their opposition*

por

Pase **por** aquí, señor	*Come this way, Sir*
por esa carretera	***along** that main road*
El agua corre **por** este tubo	*Water runs **through** this pipe*
Llegamos a Barcelona **por** Zaragoza	*We reached Barcelona **via** Zaragoza*
Di un paseo **por** nuestro barrio	*I took a stroll **around/through** our neighbourhood*
Pasa **por** mi despacho todos los días	*He drops **into** my office every day*
Ella anda **por** aquí/**por** allí	*She's **around** here/**out** there somewhere*
Miré **por** la ventana	*I looked **out of** the window*
El agua goteaba **por** las paredes	*The water was dripping **down** the walls*
Mandan el paquete **por** tren/barco	*They're sending the packet **by** train/boat*
Ella me llamó **por** teléfono	*She phoned me (She called me **by** phone)*
Conducía a cien kilómetros **por** hora	*He was driving at 100 kms **an** hour*
cinco clases **por** día	*five classes **a** day/**per** day*
Ella vendía la tela **por** metro	*She was selling the cloth **by** the metre*
¿Qué recibiste **por** el anillo?	*What did you get **(in exchange) for** the ring?*
Lo pagaré **por** entregas	*I'll pay for it **by** instalments*
Fue atacado **por** un oso	*He was attacked **by** a bear*
diez multiplicado/dividido **por** cinco	*ten multiplied/divided **by** five*

¿**Por** qué?	*Why? (=* ***For*** *what reason?)*
por todo lo que me has contado	***judging by*** *all that you've told me*
Eché una siesta **por** la tarde	*I had a nap* ***in*** *the afternoon*
Sólo viene **por** un mes	*He's only coming* ***for*** *a month*
por un lado, **por** otro lado	***on*** *the one hand,* ***on*** *the other hand*
por una parte, **por** otra parte	***on*** *the one hand,* ***on*** *the other hand*
por todos lados	***on*** *all sides*
por todas partes	*everywhere*
ropa **por** lavar	*clothes* ***(waiting/still) to*** *be washed*
Empecé **por** reír, pero terminé **por** llorar	*I started out laughing, but I ended up crying*
Recibí el recado **por** un amigo	*I got the message* ***through*** *a friend*
¿Me toma Vd. **por** simple?	*Do you take me* ***for*** *a fool?*
Yo no quería hacerlo **por** miedo	*I didn't want to do it* ***out of*** *fear*
No fuimos **por** falta de dinero	*We didn't go* ***for/through*** *lack of money*
su respeto **por** la ley	*his respect* ***for*** *the law*
su amor **por** su novio	*her love* ***for*** *her fiancé*
por la patria	***for (the sake of)*** *one's homeland*
Ella hablará **por** su padre	*She will speak* ***for (on behalf of)*** *her father*
¡No lo hagas **por** mí!	*Don't do it* ***on*** *my* ***account!***
Por mí me da igual	***As far as*** *I'm* ***concerned*** *it's all the same*
No ganará, **por** listo que sea	*He won't win,* ***however*** *clever he is*
No ganará, **por** bien que lo haga	*He won't win,* ***however*** *well he does it*

con rumbo a

con rumbo a Madrid	***in the direction of/on the way to*** *Madrid*

según

según las fuentes oficiales ...	***according to*** *official sources ...*
Varía **según** la hora	*It varies* ***depending on*** *the time of day*

sin

sin equipaje	***without any*** *luggage*
Lo haré **sin** tu ayuda	*I'll do it* ***without*** *your help*
agua mineral **sin** gas	***un****carbonated mineral water*
Ella salió **sin** decir ni una palabra	*She went out* ***without*** *(uttering) a word*
varios libros **sin** leer	*several* ***un****read books*

sobre

pétalos **sobre** la superficie del agua	*petals* ***upon/on*** *the surface of the water*
Lo puse **sobre** la mesa	*I put it* ***on/onto*** *the table*
el piso **sobre** el nuestro	*the flat* ***above/over*** *ours*
La pelota pasó **sobre** mi cabeza	*The ball went/flew* ***over/above*** *my head*
un informe **sobre** el problema	*a report* ***on/about*** *the problem*
Saldré de la biblioteca **sobre** las ocho	*I'll leave the library* ***around/about*** *eight*

tras

Está allí, **tras** el sofá	*It's there,* ***behind*** *the sofa*
noche **tras** noche	*night* ***after*** *night*

PRONOUNS (LOS PRONOMBRES)

SUBJECT PRONOUNS (LOS PRONOMBRES PERSONALES DE SUJETO)

There are a total of twelve of these, counting masculine and feminine forms:

yo	**tú**	**Vd.**	**él**	**ella**	**nosotros, -as**	**vosotros, -as**	**Vds.**	**ellos**	**ellas**
I	*you*	*you*	*he, it*	*she, it*	*we (m, f)*	*you (m, f)*	*you (pl)*	*they (m, f)*	

When using these pronouns remember that:

1. Subject pronouns are required in English whereas in Spanish they are not. They are normally omitted in Spanish if it is clear from the verb ending and/or the context who is the subject of the verb.
   As a result, Spanish subject pronouns therefore tend to be used only to avoid ambiguity, and also for emphasis.

   Example: Dibuja bien ***He*** or ***She*** or ***You*** *(formal) draw(s) well* (ambiguity)
   Ella dibuja bien ***She*** *draws well* (no ambiguity)

   Admiro a mi tío; sobre todo toca el piano muy bien
   I admire my uncle; above all ***he*** *plays the piano very well*
   (no ambiguity thanks to the context, so no subject pronoun is necessary)

   Tú no debes decir nada; **yo** hablaré con el policía
   You *should not say anything;* ***I*** *shall speak with the policeman* (emphasis)

2. **Tú** is used when speaking to **one person** you know well, to a member of the family, to a child or to a pet.

3. **Vosotros, -as** is the plural of **tú** and is used when speaking to **two or more people** you know well, etc. **Vosotros** is used to refer to all-masculine or mixed groups, **vosotras** to refer to all-feminine groups.

4. **Usted** (shortened forms **Ud.** or **Vd.**) is used when speaking to **one adult** you do not know very well (to show respect), and takes the **third** person singular of the verb.
   Example: **Vd.** acaba de llegar, ¿verdad? ***You*** *have just arrived, haven't you?*

5. **Ustedes** (shortened forms **Uds.** or **Vds.**) is used when speaking to two or more adults you do not know very well, and takes the **third** person plural of the verb.
   Example: Todos **ustedes** dormirán aquí *All of* ***you*** *will sleep here*

6. Like **vosotros, -as**, the pronouns **nosotros** and **ellos** are used to refer to all-masculine or mixed groups, **nosotras** and **ellas** to refer to all-feminine groups.
   Example: Aquí estuvieron Pablo y Marta. - ¿Qué querían **ellos**?
   "Pablo and Marta were here." "What did ***they*** *want?"*
   - **Nosotras** tendremos que hacer algo, dijo Dolores a sus dos amigas
   *"****We*** *shall have to do something", Dolores said to her two (female) friends*

7. *It* and *they* as subject pronouns referring to inanimate objects have no equivalents in Spanish and are always to be inferred from the verb.

Example:	¿Te gusta la paella?	- Sí, sabe a azafrán
	"Do you like the paella?"	*"Yes, **it** tastes of saffron"*
	¿Te dieron las máquinas nuevas?	- Sí, funcionan muy bien
	"Did they give you the new machines?"	*"Yes, **they** work very well"*

Further Uses for Subject Pronouns

1. A few prepositions combine with subject pronouns rather than with the more common prepositional pronouns (see page 55):

entre	entre yo y tú	*between me and you*
	entre nosotros	*among us/between us*
según	según tú	*according to you*
	según ellos	*according to them*
hasta	hasta yo	*even I/even me*
incluso	incluso tú	*including you*
excepto	excepto ellas	*except them*
menos	menos tú	*except you*
salvo	salvo vosotros	*except you*

2. To render the phrase *it's me, it's us*, etc, Spanish uses the appropriate person of the verb **ser** plus the subject pronoun:
   Example: Soy **yo** *It's me* Somos **nosotros** *It's us* Eran **ellos** *It was them*

3. Subject pronouns are also used as the one-word answer to a question:
   Example: ¿Quién quiere más helado? ¡**Yo**!
   *Who wants more ice-cream? **I** do!*

4. When making comparisons:
   Example: Mi hermano es más activo que **yo**
   *My brother is more active than **I (am)**/than **me***

5. In composite subjects:
   Example: **Tú** y **yo**, iremos al circo mañana
   ***You** and **I** will go to the circus tomorrow*

6 Repetition of the subject pronoun can emphasize it:
   Example: Yo suelo ir a pie, pero **él,** él siempre conduce
   *I usually go on foot, but **he** always drives*

7. Subject pronouns can also be combined with **mismo, -a, -os, -as**:
   Example: Lo he hecho **yo mismo**
   I** did it **myself
   Nosotros mismos podríamos participar
   ***We ourselves** could participate*

OBJECT PRONOUNS (LOS PRONOMBRES PERSONALES DE COMPLEMENTO)

There are three types of object pronoun: direct, indirect and reflexive.

Direct:	**me**	**te**	**lo (le)***	**la**	**nos**	**os**	**los (les)***	**las**
	me	*you*	*him, it (you)*	*her, it (you)*	*us*	*you*	*them (m) (you)*	*them (f) (you)*

* **Le(s)** is sometimes used in place of **lo(s)** when a masculine person or persons (but not a thing or things) is being referred to.

These pronouns are used when the person or thing is the direct recipient of the verb action:

Example:	¿**Me** oyes?	*Do/Can you hear **me**?*
	Ella **los** guiará **a Vds.**	*She will guide **you*** (formal)
	Los voy a comprar	*I'm going to buy **them*** (inanimate)
	Nos miran	*They are watching/looking at **us***

Note: just as **usted/ustedes** combine with third person singular/plural verbs, so likewise their equivalent direct object pronouns are in the third person - **lo, la, los, las**.

Note: personal "a" + noun is a direct object, and therefore requires a direct object pronoun
Example: Vi a su madre; **la** conozco bien *I saw his mother; I know her well*

Indirect: These express the Genitive and Dative ideas *of, to, at, on, for* and *from*:

me	*of, to, at, on, for, from me*
te	*of, to, at, on, for, from you*
le	*of, to, at, on, for, from him, her, it, (you)*
nos	*of, to, at, on, for, from us*
os	*of, to, at, on, for, from you*
les	*of, to, at, on, for, from them, (you)*

Example:	Ella **me** habla	*She speaks **to me***
	A Vds. les ofrecen un regalo	*They are offering **you** (= **to** you) a present*
	Les tenemos miedo	*We are afraid **of them***
	Os dirigen sus críticas	*They are directing their criticisms **at** you*
	Me echan la culpa	*They're putting the blame **on** me*
	Te han comprado un libro	*They have bought a book **for/from you*** (meaning determined by context)

Reflexive:	**me**	**te**	**se**	**nos**	**os**	**se**
	myself	*yourself*	*him-, her-, oneself (yourself)*	*ourselves*	*yourselves*	*themselves (yourselves)*

These refer back to the subject of the verb, so that the subject and the direct or indirect object pronoun are the same.

Example:	¿Por qué **te** rascabas?	*Why were you scratching **yourself**?*
	Me afeito	*I'm shaving **(myself)***
	¿**Se** maquilló Vd.?	*Have you put make-up on? **(yourself)***
	Ella **se** cepilla los dientes	*She is brushing her **(own)** teeth **(herself)***

Position of the Pronoun in the Sentence

Having decided which pronoun you need, the next consideration is its position in the sentence.

The direct object pronoun (DOP), the indirect object pronoun (IOP) and the reflexive pronoun (RP) normally come immediately **before** the verb, either the main verb in simple tenses or the auxiliary verb in compound tenses.

Example:

DOP	**Me** perseguían	*They were pursuing **me***
	Los habías perdido	*You had lost **them***
IOP	Ella **me** entregó el dinero	*She handed the money over **to me***
	Nos han servido la comida	*They have served the meal **to us***
RP	**Se** sentó en la silla	*He sat down (seated **himself**) on the chair*
	Os habéis divertido mucho	*You have had a good time* (literally *You have amused **yourselves** a lot*)

Exceptions to the general rule

The above holds true **except** when the direct object pronoun, the indirect object pronoun or the reflexive pronoun is in combination with the infinitive, the gerund, or the affirmative imperative, when the pronoun is normally attached to the **end** of the verbal form.

Example:

DOP	Acabar**lo** es difícil	*Finishing **it** is difficult*
	trayéndo**los** a casa	*bringing **them** home*
	Déja**me** en paz	*Leave **me** in peace*
IOP	Es un placer escribir**te** cartas	*Writing **you** letters is a pleasure*
	hablándo**nos**	*speaking **to us***
	Hága**me** el favor de ...	*Do **me** the favour of ...*
RP	Comportar**se** bien es fácil	*Behaving (Conducting **oneself**) well is easy*
	duchándo**se**	*taking a shower*
	¡Agárren**se** todos!	*Everyone hold on tight!*
but:	No **me** abandones aquí	*Don't leave **me** here* (DOP)
	No **le** quites el juguete	*Don't take the toy away **from him*** (IOP)
	No **se** queje Vd.	*Don't (you) complain* (RP)

Alternative positions with the infinitive and the gerund

However, in cases where the infinitive or the gerund (but **not** the imperative) are part of a larger verb structure, the direct object pronoun, the indirect object pronoun or the reflexive pronoun can **either** precede the first verb **or** be attached to the end of the infinitive or gerund.

Example:

DOP	quiero acabar**lo**	or	**lo** quiero acabar
	está trayéndo**los**	or	**los** está trayendo
IOP	voy a escribir**te**	or	**te** voy a escribir
	Estaban hablándo**nos**	or	**Nos** estaban hablando
RP	debes comportar**te** bien	or	**te** debes comportar bien
	¿Puedo duchar**me**?	or	¿**Me** puedo duchar?

ORDER OF PRONOUNS

If you have more than one pronoun in a sentence, the usual order can be set out in table form as follows and you can pick one from each column.

1	2	3	4	5	6	7
subject	**negative**	**reflexive**	**indirect**	**direct**	**VERB†**	**negative**
yo		me§	me	me§		
tú		te§	te	te§		
Vd.		se	le/se*	lo/la		nunca/ jamás/
él/ella	no	se	le/se*	lo/la		nadie/ nada/
nosotros, -as		nos§	nos	nos§		tampoco/ más/
vosotros, -as		os§	os	os§		ni ... ni .../ etc
Vds.		se	les/se*	los/las		
ellos/ellas		se	les/se*	los/las		

§ see the section on Exceptions below.

* when indirect and direct object pronouns both in the third person are combined in the same phrase, the indirect pronoun changes from **le/les** to **se**.

† remember that pronouns are attached to the end of the infinitive, the gerund and the affirmative imperative, and two or more pronouns are run together; the same rules of order apply, except that in these cases the verb comes **before** the pronoun or pronouns.

As there is often considerable scope for confusion when using third person pronouns, phrases such as **a él**, **a ella**, **a Vd.**, **a ellos**, etc are often appended to clarify the meaning.

Examples:

Se me ha averiado el coche — *My car has broken down **on me***
(3 + 4 + 6)

Se le prohibe entrar — *He is forbidden to enter*
(3 + 4 + 6)

Nosotras **nos los** pusimos — *We (women, girls) put **them** (eg shoes, hats) on*
(1 + 3 + 5 + 6)

No **os lo** darán jamás — *They will never give **it to you** (pl)*
(2 + 4 + 5 + 6 + 7)

Ella no **me las** ha recomendado — *She has not recommended **them** (f pl) **to me***
(1 + 2 + 4 + 5 + 6)

Se lo prometo **a Vds.** — *I promise **you (it)***
(4* + 5 + 6)

Y las joyas, ¿**se las** vendiste **a él**? *And the jewels, did you sell **them to him**?*
(4* + 5 + 6)

¿No vas a mandár**melos** nunca? *Aren't you ever going to send **them to me**?*
(2 + 6 + 4 + 5 + 7)

Me he cansado describiéndo**tela** *I have exhausted **myself** describing **her to you***
(3 + 6; 6 + 4 + 5)

Lléve**selo (a ellos)** — *Take **it to them** (m)*
(6 + 4* + 5)

Exceptions:

When a direct object pronoun or a reflexive pronoun in the first or second persons (me§, te§, nos§, os§) is combined with an indirect object pronoun, they cannot both appear before the verb, and so the indirect object pronoun is replaced with a prepositional phrase.

Example:	**Me** describieron **a ti**	*They described **me to you***
	Te describieron **a mí**	*They described **you to me***
	Nos describimos **a ti**	*We described **ourselves to you***
Compare:	**Me** describieron a mis parientes	*They described **me** to my relatives*
	Te describieron a Mario [personal "a"]	*They described Mario **to you***
	Nos describimos a María	*We described **ourselves** to Maria*

Prepositional Pronouns (Los Pronombres Preposicionales)

mí	**ti**	**Vd.**	**él**	**ella**	**sí**
me, myself	*you, yourself*	*you*	*him*	*her*	*him/her/itself, yourself*
nosotros, -as	**vosotros, -as**	**Vds.**	**ellos**	**ellas**	**sí**
us, ourselves	*you, yourselves*	*you (pl)*	*them (m)*	*them (f)*	*themselves, yourselves*

1. As their name implies, these pronouns are used after prepositions:
   Example: para **mí**, sin **Vd.**, en **sí**, alrededor de **vosotros**, cerca de **ellas**

   Note that the forms **a él, de él** are **not** the same as preposition + definite article (**al, del**) and hence they do **not** merge into one word:
   Example: **se** lo enviaré **a él**, no a ti — *I'll send it to him, not to you*
   de él he oído las noticias — *I've heard the news from him*

2. The preposition **con** is a partial exception: it creates the forms **conmigo** (*with me/myself*), **contigo** (*with you/yourself*) and **consigo** (*with himself, herself*, etc). It behaves normally with all the other pronouns: **con él, con vosotras, con Vds.**, etc.

3. Prepositional pronouns, often with an appropriate preposition (**a**), are used to emphasize the object pronoun:
   Example: **A mí** me gusta la música clásica, pero mis amigos prefieren el jazz
   I like classical music, but my friends prefer jazz

4. Prepositional pronouns are often combined with **mismo, -a, -os, -as**:
   Example: Sólo aceptaré el recado de **ti mismo**
   *I will only accept the message from **you yourself***
   Ellos no podían cuidarse a **sí mismos**
   *They could not take care of **themselves***

5. **Ello**, meaning *it* or *that*, is used in conjunction with a preposition to refer back to a concept or topic already established. It is **not** used to refer to concrete nouns which, according to their gender, require **él** or **ella**.
   Example: ¿Por qué sigues hablando de **ello**?
   *Why do you keep on talking about **it**?*

RELATIVE PRONOUNS (LOS PRONOMBRES RELATIVOS)

These are: **que**, *who, whom, which, that*, **quien, -es**, *who, whom, that*, and **cuyo, -a, -os, -as**, *whose*. **Que** is used **both** of people and things. **Quien** is used exclusively with people. It cannot be used to introduce identifying clauses but it can be used in descriptive clauses (normally enclosed between commas); when combined with prepositions - a **quien, de quienes**, etc - it tends to be more common. **Cuyo** is used for people and things.

These pronouns are used to introduce a clause which is giving more information about a noun. You must select the correct relative pronoun according to its grammatical function within the clause.

1. The relative pronoun can be the subject of the clause:

Example: La señora **que** canta es mi tía (identifying - **que** only)
*The lady **who** is singing is my aunt*
Esa señora, **que/quien** es cantante, es mi tía (descriptive - **que** or **quien**)
*That lady, **who** is a singer, is my aunt*
Los guantes **que** están en la mesa son míos
*The gloves (**which are**) on the table are mine*

2. The relative pronoun can be the direct object of the main verb. Note that clauses of this type will contain a different subject in the form of a noun or pronoun:

Example: El chico **que/a quien** Cristóbal vio en el parque ...
*The boy **who(m)** Cristóbal saw in the park ...*
Mis amigas **que/a quienes** ayudo a menudo
*My friends **who(m)** I frequently help*
El trabajo **que** hago es muy difícil
*The work (**that**) I am doing is very hard*

Notice that **quien** requires the personal "a" while **que** does not.

3. The relative pronoun can be the indirect object of the clause.

Example: He aquí la persona **a quien** di el billete
*Here is the person **to whom** I gave the ticket/I gave the ticket to*
Éste es el banco **al que** mando todo mi dinero
*This is the bank **to which** I send all my money*

The relative pronoun for an indirect object that is a person can **only** be **quien**. As usual, the relative pronoun for a thing is **que**, but notice that when it is an indirect object it requires the preposition **a**. **Take care** not to confuse the true indirect object construction with the direct object personal "a" construction.

The relative pronoun in Spanish can **never** be left out, as it sometimes can in English.

Example: *The woman I saw*
must be translated as La mujer **que/a quien** vi

The business I gave the money to
must be translated as La empresa **a que** di el dinero

Notice also that while in English it is quite common to have a "dangling" preposition: *the business I gave the money **to***, in Spanish the preposition **must** come before the relative pronoun: la empresa **a que** di el dinero.

4. The relative pronoun can mean *of whom, of which (that)*:

Example: los niños **de quienes** te burlabas
*the children **of whom** you were making fun/you were making fun of*
la guerra **de que** se cuentan mil cosas
*the war **of which** a thousand things are told*

5. The relative pronoun can mean *whose*:

Example: esa casa **cuyo** techo está cubierto de hojas
*that house **whose** roof is covered with leaves*
este acróbata de **cuyas** habilidades nos han hablado tantas veces
*this acrobat of **whose** skills they have spoken to us so many times*

Notice that **cuyo, cuya, cuyos, cuyas** agrees with the noun it precedes and governs, **not** with the person or thing to whom that noun belongs.

More Relative Pronouns

El cual, la cual, los cuales, las cuales or the alternative **el que, la que, los que, las que** also mean *who, whom, which, that.*

1. They are typically used when the relative pronoun is separated from the noun to which it refers and/or when there is room for ambiguity.

Example: la esposa de mi amigo, **la cual** quiere mudarse de casa
*the wife of my friend, **who** wants to move house*
(**que** or **quien** could refer to esposa **or** amigo, **la cual** clearly identifies esposa)
la universidad de **la que** se espera que yo reciba un diploma
*the university from **which** it is hoped that I shall receive a diploma*

2. As we have seen above, the prepositions **a** and **de** are used in combination with the common relative pronouns **que** and **quien, -es**, and this is true also of **con** and **en**.

Example: Conozco a la chica **con quien** fuiste al concierto
*I know the girl **with whom** you went to the concert*
La situación **en que** me encuentro es muy delicada
*The situation **in which** I find myself is very delicate*

Note that **en que** referring to place can often be rendered by **donde** or **en donde** and that **en que** referring to time can often be rendered by **cuando**.

Example: La ciudad **en que/donde** vives es muy agradable
*The city **in which/where** you live is very pleasant*
¿No puedes decirme la fecha **en que/cuando** ganaste el concurso?
*Can't you tell me the date **on which/when** you won the competition?*

3. However, **all** prepositions can combine with **el cual**, etc or **el que**, etc, and as usual the relative pronouns always agree.

Example: la montaña **encima de la cual** volaba un águila
*the mountain **above which** an eagle was flying*
las vías de comunicación **por las que** podremos hablarnos
*the channels of communication **through which** we shall be able to talk*

4. When referring back to the overall idea expressed in the main clause, the neuter forms **lo cual** or **lo que** are used to express *which*:

Example: Había aplastado todas las flores, **lo cual/lo que** iba a enfadar al jardinero
*He had flattened all the flowers, **which** was going to anger the gardener*
Mi tío fuma mucho, por **lo cual/lo que** mi primo no entrará en su casa
*My uncle smokes a lot, for **which reason** my cousin won't enter his house*

5. **El que, la que, los que, las que** also mean *the one(s) who, the one(s) which/that, those who, those which/that.* Note that you **cannot** use **el cual,** etc, in this sense.

Example: Esas cintas son **las que** voy a llevar esta noche
*Those ribbons are **the ones (that)** I am going to wear tonight*
¿Cuál de ellos te gustó más? - **El que** me compró una rosa
*Which one of them did you like most? - **The one who** bought me a rose*

Note: when **el que, los que**, etc means *he who, those who*, **quien, quienes** is an alternative:
Example: **Quienes** (**Los que**) quieran entrar, que lo hagan ahora
***Those who** want to go in, please do so now*

6. **Lo que**, *what, the thing that*, is the neuter form of the above and usually refers to a general concept or topic. Note again that you **cannot** use **lo cual** in this sense.

Example: **Lo que** se propone no nos ayudará nada (subject)
***What** is being proposed will not help us at all*
Me dijo **lo que** le habías escrito (direct object)
*He told me **what** you had written to him*
Ella no sabe nada de **lo que** me dijiste (preposition + pronoun)
*She knows nothing of **what** you told me*

In indirect questions (a sentence in which a question is being asked but there is no question mark), **lo que** and **qué** (with an accent) are alternatives.
Example: Te van a preguntar **lo que/qué** has estado haciendo
*They are going to ask you **what** you have been doing*

7. **Todos, -as** can be added to the plural **los/las que** and **todo** to the neuter form **lo que**.

Example: **Todos los que** necesiten servicio tendrán que esperar
***All those who** need service will have to wait*
¿Cuántas gambas podemos comer? - **Todas las que** queráis
*How many prawns can we eat? - **As many as** you like/**All** you like*
He tomado apuntes detallados de **todo lo que** has dicho
*I have taken detailed notes of **all that** you have said*

8. **El <u>de</u>, la <u>de</u>, los <u>de</u>, las <u>de</u>** are used to translate *the one(s) of, that/those of.*

Example: Corrigió mi ejercicio y **el de** mi amigo
He corrected my exercise and my friend's (the one of my friend)
Asistirán las familias de aquí y **las del** extranjero
*The families from here and **those from abroad** will attend*

Imagine that the noun is repeated in the second half of the phrase - **mi ejercicio y <u>el</u> (ejercicio) de mi amigo** - and then that the noun is omitted again. The correct article for the noun (in this case **el**) will always give you the correct relative pronoun.

INTERROGATIVE PRONOUNS (LOS PRONOMBRES INTERROGATIVOS)

These pronouns ask questions: *who?, what?, which one?, how much?, how many?*

1. When talking about **people:**

If the word *who?* is the subject of the verb, you use either **¿quién?** or **¿quiénes?**
Example: **¿Quién** ha llegado? ***Who** has arrived?*

If the word *who(m)?* is the object of the verb you use **¿a quién?** or **¿a quiénes?**
Example: **¿A quién** viste? ***Who(m)** did you see?*

If the pronoun is used with prepositions you use ¿preposition + **quién, -es?**
Example: **¿Con quiénes** estás hablando? ***Who** are you talking to?*
¿De quién es esta radio? ***Whose** is this radio?*

2. When talking about **things**:

If the word *what*? is the subject of the verb, you use **¿Qué?**
Example: **¿Qué** te interesa? ***What** interests you?*

If *what* is the object of the verb, you again use **¿Qué?**
Example: **¿Qué** haces allí? ***What** are you doing there?*

If *what* is used with a preposition, you use ¿preposition + **qué?**
Example: **¿En qué** piensas? ***What** are you thinking **of/about**?*
¿Para qué haces eso? ***What** are you doing that **for**?*
but note: **¿Por qué** gritas tanto? ***Why** are you shouting so much?*

3. When wanting to know *Which one(s)?*, **¿Cuál?, ¿Cuáles?** are used:

Example: -Vi a una de tus amigas ayer. -¿Verdad? **¿A cuál?**
*"I saw one of your friends yesterday." "Really? **Which one**?"*
¿Cuál de estas tres bufandas es la tuya?
***Which (one)** of these three scarves is yours?*
-Fuimos a muchos lugares. -**¿Cuáles** os gustaron más?
*"We went to many places". "**Which ones** did you like best?"*

4. **¿Cuál?, ¿Cuáles?** are also generally used before **ser** *to be*, because **¿Qué?** before **ser** means *What is the nature of?*

   Example: **¿Cuál** es la capital de China? *What's the capital of China?*
   ¿Cuál fue el resultado? *What was the result?*
   ¿Cuáles son las razones? *What are the reasons?*
   but **¿Qué** es una promesa? *What is (the nature of) a promise?*

5. When wanting to know *How much?/How many?*, **¿Cuánto?, ¿Cuántos?, ¿Cuántas?** are used:

   Example: **¿Cuánto** necesitas? ***How much** do you need?*
   ¿Cuánto vale? ***How much** is it/does it cost?*
   ¿Cuántos crees que puedes terminar hoy?
   ***How many** do you think you can finish today?*

6. All of these interrogative pronouns will also work in indirect questions, that is sentences that contain a reported question and do not end with a question mark:

   Example: Quiero saber **con quién** has estado y **qué** has hecho
   *I want to know **with whom** you've been and **what** you have done*

Demonstrative Pronouns (Los Pronombres Demostrativos)

These include:

	this one, these ones	*that one, those ones*	*that one, those ones*
ms	**éste**	**ése**	**aquél**
fs	**ésta**	**ésa**	**aquélla**
mpl	**éstos**	**ésos**	**aquéllos**
fpl	**éstas**	**ésas**	**aquéllas**
neuter	**esto**	**eso**	**aquello**

1. The three neuter pronouns refer to an unspecified thing, concept or topic:

   Example: ¡Mira **esto**! *Look at **this**!*
   ¿Has visto **eso**? *Did you see **that**?*
   Aquello es lo que nos espera ***That**'s what's waiting for us*

   Note: the neuter forms do **not** have a written accent, as there is no corresponding demonstrative adjective from which they need to be distinguished.

2. All the other demonstrative pronouns are chosen according to the number and gender of the noun to which they refer. The differentiation between **ése** and **aquél** is exactly the same as with the corresponding demonstrative adjectives. (See page 16)

   Example: ¿Qué árbol? **Éste** que está cerca de la casa
   *What tree? **This one** which is close to the house*
   Estas manzanas están más maduras que **ésas**
   *These apples are riper than **those***
   Estas montañas son menos altas que **aquéllas** más lejanas
   *These mountains are less high than **those** further away*
   ¿Cuáles libros quieres? **Éste** y **aquél**
   *Which books do you want? **This one here** and **that one over there***

3. A further use for **aquél, aquélla**, etc and **éste, ésta**, etc is to designate *the former* and *the latter.* A good way to remember which is which is that in any sentence *the former* comes first and is therefore "further away" (=**aquél**) when you need to refer back to it later in the sentence.

Example: Ricardo y María andaban por el camino; **aquél** iba con un bastón y **ésta** tenía unos gemelos
*Ricardo and Maria were walking along the path; **the former** had a walking stick and **the latter** had a pair of binoculars*

Possessive Pronouns (Los Pronombres Posesivos)

These are the words which mean *mine, yours, his, hers, its, ours, yours, theirs.*

They are as follows:

ms	fs	mpl	fpl	Meaning
one owner, one object owned		**one owner, several objects owned**		
el mío	la mía	los míos	las mías	*mine*
el tuyo	la tuya	los tuyos	las tuyas	*yours*
el suyo	la suya	los suyos	las suyas	*his/hers/its/yours*
2+ owners, one object owned		**2+ owners, several objects owned**		
el nuestro	la nuesta	los nuestros	las nuestras	*ours*
el vuestro	la vuestra	los vuestros	las vuestras	*yours*
el suyo	la suya	los suyos	las suyas	*theirs/yours*

The form used will vary according to the gender and number of the noun referred to. **Choice of gender depends on the gender of the object owned, not the sex of the owner:**

Example: -Éste es tu abrigo. ¿Dónde está **el mío**?, preguntó ella
*"This is your coat. Where's **mine**?", she asked*
Cristina ha encontrado tu peine pero no puede encontrar **el suyo**
*Cristina has found your comb but cannot find **hers***
Entre todos estos juguetes no sé cuáles son **los míos**
*Among all these toys I don't know which ones are **mine***
Mi prima es muy inteligente pero **la tuya** es un genio
*My cousin (f) is very intelligent but **yours** (f) is a genius*
De todos los yates en el lago todavía preferimos **el nuestro**
*Of all the yachts on the lake we still prefer **ours***
Doy hierba a mi conejillo de Indias; ¿qué dáis **al vuestro**?
*I give grass to my guinea pig; what do you give to **yours**?*
Ella admira a mi padre pero no sé qué piensa **del suyo**
*She admires my father but I don't know what she thinks of **hers/her own***

Indefinite Pronouns (Los Pronombres Indefinidos)

Here are some common indefinite pronouns, together with examples of how to use them:

algo	Tenemos que hacer **algo** *We have to do **something***
alguien	Tranquilízate; **alguien** nos ayudará *Calm down; **someone** will help us*
alguno, -a, -os, -as	No tengo lápices en casa así que tendré que comprar **algunos** *I don't have any pencils in the house so I'll have to buy **some***
cada uno, cada una	Voy a darles un dulce a **cada uno/cada una** *I'm going to give a sweet to **each one** (of them)*
cualquiera	**Cualquiera** de mis alumnos lo haría mejor ***Any one** of my pupils would do that better*
los/las demás	Hay que dejar un trozo del pastel para **los demás** *A piece of the cake should be left for **the others***
mucho, -a, -os, -as	Leo una novela cada día pero no tengo **muchas** aquí *I read a novel every day but I don't have **many** here*
nada	¿Qué hay en la caja? - **Nada** *"What is there in the box?" "**Nothing**"*
nadie	**Nadie** querría limpiar esta casa ***No-one** would want to clean this house*
ninguno, -a	Aunque tengo muchos amigos hoy no he visto a **ninguno** *Although I have many friends, today I've **not** seen **one** (of them)*
poco, -a, -os, -as	De los globos de la fiesta sólo quedan **pocos** intactos *Of the balloons from the party only **a few** are still intact*
tanto, -a, -os, -as	Cada socio tiene que contribuir **tanto** *Each member has to contribute **so much** (=a certain amount)* Era aficionado a las rosas pero nunca había visto **tantas** *He was a rose enthusiast but he had never seen **so many***
todo, -a, -os, -as	Lo vi **todo**, y por eso ella quería que se lo contara **todo** *I saw **it all**, and so she wanted me to tell her **everything*** Ella nos vio a **todos** *She saw us **all/all** of us*
varios, -as	Me gustan los periódicos; por eso suelo comprar **varios** *I like newspapers, so I usually buy **several***

VERBS - WHICH TENSE SHOULD I USE?

VERBS - BASIC CATEGORIES

All verbs in Spanish, both regular and irregular ones, fall into one of three basic families or categories; the technical name for these categories is conjugations. All verbs can be recognised and categorized by the last two letters of their infinitive form:

baj**ar** corr**er** part**ir**

These letters, **-ar, -er** or **-ir**, give the clue to the pattern that the verbs will follow in all of their tenses, ie throughout their conjugation.

PRESENT TENSE (EL TIEMPO PRESENTE)

Use of the Present Tense

This is the tense which is used to talk and write about:

- events which are taking place at this moment in time
- events which take place regularly and/or repeatedly
- events in the near future which are certain

It is also used:

- with **desde hace** and with **acabar de**

Notice that there are **three** forms of the present tense in English but only **two** in Spanish:

I help, I do help: - both of these are translated by **ayudo**
I am helping: - which is translated by **estoy ayudando** (**estar** + gerund)
He watches, he does watch: - both of these are translated by **mira**
He is watching: - which is translated by **está mirando** (**estar** + gerund)

Spanish has different verb endings for **each** person and number in the present tense.

The **Continuous or Progressive Present**, *I am helping, he is watching*, is formed with the appropriate person and tense of the auxiliary verb **estar**, and will be treated below. Note that other auxiliary verbs can also be combined with the gerund, such as **andar, ir, venir**:

Example: voy cantando *I am going along singing*

Spanish normally omits the subject pronoun unless there is ambiguity or emphasis is required, so the standard translation for *I help* is **ayudo**.
The English auxiliary *do, does* is **included** in the normal verb form.

FORMATION OF THE PRESENT TENSE

1. Verbs with Infinitive in -ar

(a) Present Tense of Regular -ar Verbs

To form the present tense of a regular **-ar** verb, for example trabaj**ar**, take away the final **-ar** of the infinitive, and then add the endings **-o, -as, -a, -amos, -áis, -an**

Trabajar - ***to work***

trabaj**o**	*I work, I do work*
trabaj**as**	*you work, you do work*
Vd. trabaj**a**	*you (formal) work, you do work*
él/ella/Manolo trabaj**a**	*he/she/Manolo works, does work*
trabaj**amos**	*we work, we do work*
trabaj**áis**	*you (pl) work, you do work*
Vds. trabaj**an**	*you (formal pl) work, you do work*
ellos/ellas trabaj**an**	*they work, they do work*
Manolo e Isabel trabaj**an**	*Manolo and Isabel work, do work*

Other common regular -ar verbs include:

admirar, alcanzar*, amar, amenazar*, avanzar*, averiguar*, ayudar, bailar, bajar, buscar*, cambiar, causar, cazar*, cenar, colocar*, comprar, copiar, desayunar, desear, dibujar, durar, echar, elogiar, emplear, empujar, entrar, entregar*, escuchar, esperar, estudiar, ganar, gastar, golpear, gritar, guardar, gustar, hablar, intentar, invitar, lanzar*, lavar, levantar, limpiar, luchar, llegar*, llenar, llevar, llorar, mandar, marchar, mirar, nadar, odiar, olvidar, pagar*, pasar, pasear, pintar, preguntar, quedar, quitar, regresar, sacar*, saltar, terminar, tocar*, tomar, tratar, viajar, visitar

* Verbs marked with an asterisk are entirely regular except for some minor spelling changes in the preterite (pages 75-76), present subjunctive (page 84) and command forms (page 88). Verbs affected are those spelt with a **-c-, -g-, -gu-** or **-z-** immediately before the **-ar** ending. These spelling changes do **not** affect the present tense in any way.

(b) Present Tense of Radical-changing -ar Verbs

Radical-changing verbs have regular endings but the vowel in the root of the verb changes in some persons and some tenses. The root is the part of the infinitive **before** the ending: eg **cerr-** is the root of **cerrar** *to close*, and **-e-** would therefore be the vowel that changes. In verbs with more than one syllable in the root, it is always the **last** syllable **just before** the infinitive ending that contains the vowel that changes:
eg **atraves-** is the root of **atravesar** *to cross*, and it is the **-e-** in the syllable **-ves-** that is the vowel that changes.
Fortunately, these changes follow predictable rules. There are two kinds of radical-changing **-ar** verbs; those with the vowel **e** and those with the vowel **o** or **u** in their root.

1. Radical-changing **-ar** verbs with root vowel **e** form the present tense by changing **e** → **ie** in all singular forms and the third person plural:

Pensar - ***to think***

p**ie**nso	*I think, I do think*
p**ie**nsas	*you think, you do think*
Vd. p**ie**nsa	*you (formal) think, you do think*
él/ella/Manolo p**ie**nsa	*he/she/Manolo thinks, does think*
pensamos	*we think, we do think*
pensáis	*you (pl) think, you do think*
Vds. p**ie**nsan	*you (formal pl) think, you do think*
ellos/ellas p**ie**nsan	*they think, they do think*
Manolo e Isabel p**ie**nsan	*Manolo and Isabel think, do think*

Other common verbs that behave like **pensar** are:

atravesar, cerrar, comenzar*, confesar, despertar, empezar*, encerrar, enterrar, gobernar, helar, manifestar, negar*, nevar, pensar, quebrar, regar*, sentar

* Verbs marked with an asterisk behave like **pensar** but, in addition, undergo some minor spelling changes in the preterite (page 76), present subjunctive (page 84) and command forms (page 88).
These spelling changes do **not** affect the present tense in any way.

2. Radical-changing **-ar** verbs with root vowel **o** or **u** form the present tense by changing **o** → **ue** or **u** → **ue** in all singular forms and the third person plural:

Mostrar - ***to show***

m**ue**stro	*I show, I do show*
m**ue**stras	*you show, you do show*
Vd. m**ue**stra	*you (formal) show, you do show*
él/ella/Manolo m**ue**stra	*he/she/Manolo shows, does show*
mostramos	*we show, we do show*
mostráis	*you (pl) show, you do show*
Vds. m**ue**stran	*you (formal pl) show, you do show*
ellos/ellas m**ue**stran	*they show, they do show*
Manolo e Isabel m**ue**stran	*Manolo and Isabel show, do show*

Other common verbs that behave like **mostrar** are:

acordar, acostar, almorzar*, colgar*, contar, costar, demostrar, encontrar, forzar*, recordar, rogar*, soltar, sonar, soñar, trocar*, volar

* Verbs marked with an asterisk behave like **mostrar** but, in addition, undergo some minor spelling changes in the preterite, present subjunctive and imperative forms (see below). These spelling changes do **not** affect the present tense in any way.

There is only one radical-changing **-ar** verb with root vowel **u**: **jugar**.
Jugar also falls into the category of verbs with minor spelling changes in certain other tenses and forms.

(c) Present Tense of Irregular -ar Verbs

The only really irregular verbs in the present tense with an infinitive ending in **-ar** are **dar** and **estar**. **Dar** is only irregular in the first person singular and second person plural of the present tense. Their conjugation is given in full in the Verb Table, pages 103-107.

SPELLING CHANGES TO OTHERWISE REGULAR VERBS (AND RADICAL-CHANGING VERBS)

Quite a number of otherwise regular verbs and radical-changing verbs undergo slight spelling changes under certain circumstances. The changes are always made to preserve the original pronunciation of the infinitive. The changes only affect certain conjugations of verbs in certain persons and in certain tenses.
For instance, regular **-ar** verbs in the present tense are entirely unaffected. Regular **-er** verbs that end in **-cer** and **-ger**, are affected but only in the first person singular. Reference will be made to these changes on a number of occasions in the course of this section, so it is as well to give the complete set of rules here.

The underlying reason for most of these changes is that there are hard vowels **(a, o, u)** and soft vowels **(e** and **i)** in Spanish:

c is pronounced **k** in front of hard vowels and like Spanish **z** in front of soft vowels:
Example: es**co**ger but **ce**der

g is pronounced **g** in front of hard vowels and like Spanish **j** in front of soft vowels:
Example: **ga**nar but co**ge**r

so verbs whose root or stem ends in **c, g, gu, qu** and **z** are those affected.

1. Verbs whose root ends in **c** change the **c** → **z** to preserve the "soft" c sound before hard vowels in verb endings.
   Example: ven**ce**r → ven**zo** (1st person singular present tense)

2. Verbs whose root ends in **c** change the **c** → **qu** to preserve the "hard" c sound before soft vowels in verb endings.
   Example: sa**ca**r → sa**qu**é (1st person singular preterite tense)

3. Verbs whose root ends in **g** change the **g** → **j** to preserve the "soft" g sound before hard vowels in verb endings.
   Example: esco**ge**r → esco**j**o (1st person singular present tense)

4. Verbs whose root ends in **g** change the **g** → **gu** (the u is silent) to preserve the "hard" g sound before soft vowels in verb endings.
   Example: pa**ga**r → pa**gu**é (1st person singular preterite tense)

5. Verbs whose root ends in **gu** change the **gu** → **g** before hard vowels in verb endings as g alone before hard vowels is all that is required.
   Example: distin**gu**ir → distin**g**o (1st person singular present tense)

6. Verbs whose root ends in **gu** change the **gu** → **gü** to show the u is pronounced before soft vowels in verb endings.
   Example: averi**gu**ar → averi**gü**é (1st person singular preterite tense)

7. Verbs whose root ends in **qu** change the **qu** → **c** before hard vowels in verb endings, because c before hard vowels is pronounced as qu.
   Example: delin**qu**ir → delin**c**o (1st person singular present tense)

8. Verbs whose root ends in **z** change the **z** → **c** before soft vowels in verb endings, because c before soft vowels is pronounced as a z.
   Example: for**z**ar → for**c**é (1st person singular preterite tense)

9. Verbs ending in **-aer, -eer, -oer, oír** and **uir**, if they followed regular patterns, would create some forms where an unstressed **i** appeared between two other vowels.
   To avoid this combination of three consecutive vowels, in such cases the **i** → **y**.
   Example: leer → le**y**ó (3rd person singular preterite tense)

2. Verbs with Infinitive in -er

(a) Present Tense of Regular -er Verbs

To form the present tense of an **-er** verb, for example vend**er**, take away the final **-er** of the infinitive, and then add the endings **-o, -es, -e, -emos, -éis, -en**

Vender - ***to sell***

vend**o**	*I sell, I do sell*
vend**es**	*you sell, you do sell*
Vd. vend**e**	*you (formal) sell, you do sell*
él/ella/Manolo vend**e**	*he/she/Manolo sells, does sell*
vend**emos**	*we sell, we do sell*
vend**éis**	*you (pl) sell, you do sell*
Vds. vend**en**	*you (formal pl) sell, you do sell*
ellos/ellas vend**en**	*they sell, they do sell*
Manolo e Isabel vend**en**	*Manolo and Isabel sell, do sell*

Other common regular **-er** verbs include:

aprender, beber, ceder, coger*, comer, comprender, convencer*, correr, coser, creer*, deber, ejercer*, escoger*, leer*, mecer*, meter, poseer*, proteger*, proveer*, responder, roer*, sorprender, temer, suceder, suspender, vencer*

* Verbs marked with an asterisk are subject to the rules governing spelling changes to otherwise regular verbs. Regular **-er** verbs affected in the present tense are those ending in **-cer** and **-ger** (rules 1 or 3, page 66). (Verbs ending in **-aer, -eer, -oer** are affected in some other tenses.)

Example: convencer → conven**z**o coger → co**j**o

(b) Present Tense of Radical-changing -er Verbs

There are two kinds of radical-changing **-er** verbs, those with the vowel **e** and those with the vowel **o** in their root.

1. Radical-changing **-er** verbs with root vowel **e** form the present tense by changing **e** → **ie** in all singular forms and the third person plural:

Perder - ***to lose***

p**ie**rdo	*I lose, I do lose*
p**ie**rdes	*you lose, you do lose*
Vd. p**ie**rde	*you (formal) lose, do lose*
él/ella/Manolo p**ie**rde	*he/she/Manolo loses, does lose*
perdemos	*we lose, we do lose*
perdéis	*you (pl) lose, you do lose*
Vds. p**ie**rden	*you (formal pl) lose, you do lose*
ellos/ellas p**ie**rden	*they lose, they do lose*
Manolo e Isabel p**ie**rden	*Manolo and Isabel lose, do lose*

Other common verbs that behave like **perder** are:

ascender, atender, defender, descender, encender, entender, extender, **querer****, verter.

** **querer** is irregular in some other tenses – see Verb Table page 105.

2. Radical-changing **-er** verbs with root vowel **o** form the present tense by changing **o** → **ue** in all singular forms and the third person plural:

Volver - *to return*

v**ue**lvo	*I return, I do return*
v**ue**lves	*you return, you do return*
Vd. v**ue**lve	*you (formal) return, you do return*
él/ella/Manolo v**ue**lve	*he/she/Manolo returns, does return*
volvemos	*we return, we do return*
volvéis	*you (pl) return, you do return*
Vds. v**ue**lven	*you (formal pl) return, you do return*
ellos/ellas v**ue**lven	*they return, they do return*
Manolo e Isabel v**ue**lven	*Manolo and Isabel return, do return*

Other common verbs that behave like **volver** are:

cocer*, conmover, demoler, devolver, disolver, doler, llover, moler, mover, poder**, retorcer*, torcer*

* Verbs marked with an asterisk behave like **volver** but, in addition, are subject to the rules (nos. 1 or 3, page 66) governing spelling changes to otherwise regular verbs. Verbs affected are those ending in **–cer**, and the only form changed is the first person singular (eg torcer → t**uer**<u>z</u>o).

** **poder** is irregular in some other tenses, see page 105.

(c) Present Tense of Irregular -er Verbs

There are quite a number of irregular **-er** verbs, but many of these are only slightly irregular. Many irregularities only affect the first person singular of the present tense.

1. Most verbs ending in **-acer, -ecer** and **-ocer** create a first person singular form which ends in **-azco, -ezco** or **-ozco** respectively. They are otherwise regular in the present tense.

   Example: nacer → n**azco** (*I am born*)
   parecer → par**ezco** (*I appear/seem, I do appear/seem*)
   conocer → con**ozco** (*I know, I do know*)

Other common verbs that behave like **nacer, parecer** and **conocer** are:

aborrecer, adormecer, agradecer, aparecer, carecer, compadecer, crecer, desaparecer, desconocer, desobedecer, establecer, favorecer, merecer, obedecer, ofrecer, padecer, permanecer, pertenecer, reconocer, yacer

Exception: **satisfacer** *to satisfy* forms its first person singular irregularly → **satisfago** but is otherwise regular in the present tense.
(See Verb Table, page 106)

2. Verbs like **caer, traer,** create a first person singular form which ends in **-igo**. They are otherwise regular in the present tense.

   Example: caer → ca**igo** *I fall* traer → tra**igo** *I bring*

Other verbs that behave like **caer** and **traer** are: atraer, distraer, raer

3. Verbs that have a unique, irregular, first person singular form but are otherwise regular in the present tense include:
caber *to fit*→ **quepo** saber *to know* → **sé**
valer *to be worth* → **valgo** poner *to put* → **pongo**
Compounds based on **poner** like **componer, disponer**, etc behave similarly.

4. **tener** *to have* is a radical-changing verb like **perder**, with the added irregularity of its first person singular form: **tengo**.

tengo	tenemos
tienes	tenéis
Vd. **tie**ne	Vds. **tie**nen
él/ella **tie**ne	ellos/ellas **tie**nen
Manolo **tie**ne	Manolo e Isabel **tie**nen

Other verbs that behave like **tener** are compound verbs formed on the same root:
contener, detener, entretener, mantener, obtener, sostener (see page 107)

5. A few very common verbs are sufficiently irregular to be given in full. The present tense conjugations of **haber, hacer, ser** and **ver** can be found in the Verb Table, pages 103-107.

3. Verbs with Infinitive in -ir

(a) Present Tense of Regular -ir Verbs

To form the present tense of an **-ir** verb, for example abr**ir**, take away the final **-ir** of the infinitive, and then add the endings **-o, -es, -e, -imos, -ís, -en**

Abrir - *to open*

abr**o**	*I open, I do open*
abr**es**	*you open, you do open*
Vd. abr**e**	*you (formal) open, you do open*
él/ella/Manolo abr**e**	*he/she/Manolo opens, does open*
abr**imos**	*we open, we do open*
abr**ís**	*you (pl) open, you do open*
Vds. abr**en**	*you (formal pl) open, you do open*
ellos/ellas abr**en**	*they open, they do open*
Manolo e Isabel abr**en**	*Manolo and Isabel open, do open*

Other common regular **-ir** verbs include:
aburrir, aplaudir, atribuir*, compartir, concluir*, constituir*, construir*, contribuir*, cubrir, cundir, delinquir*, descubrir, destruir*, dirigir*, disminuir*, distinguir*, distribuir*, escribir, esparcir*, fingir*, huir*, imprimir, incluir*, influir*, partir, percibir, prohibir, recibir, sufrir, sustituir*, vivir, zurcir*

* Verbs marked with an asterisk are subject to the rules governing spelling changes to otherwise regular verbs. Regular **-ir** verbs affected in the present tense are those ending in **-cir** (rule 1), **-gir** (rule 3), **-guir** (rule 5), **-quir** (rule 7), and **-oír** and **-uir** (rule 9). See rules on page 66.

Most of these changes only affect the first person singular, but the added **-y-** (rule 9, page 66) affects all the singulars and the third person plural:

Example **Concluir** - *to conclude*:

concluyo	concluimos
concluyes	concluís
Vd. concluye	Vds. concluyen
él/ella concluye	ellos/ellas concluyen
Manolo concluye	Manolo e Isabel concluyen

(b) Present Tense of Radical-changing -ir Verbs

There are four kinds of radical-changing **-ir** verbs, three with the vowel **e** and one with the vowel **o** in their root.

1a. A few radical-changing **-ir** verbs with root vowel **e** form the present tense by changing **e** → **ie** in all singular forms and the third person plural:

Discernir - ***to discern***

disc**ie**rno	*I discern, I do discern*
disc**ie**rnes	*you discern, you do discern*
Vd. disc**ie**rne	*you (formal) discern, you do discern*
él/ella/Manolo disc**ie**rne	*he/she/Manolo discerns, does discern*
discernimos	*we discern, we do discern*
discernís	*you (pl)discern, you do discern*
Vds. disc**ie**rnen	*you (formal pl) discern, you do discern*
ellos/ellas disc**ie**rnen	*they discern, they do discern*
Manolo e Isabel disc**ie**rnen	*Manolo and Isabel discern, do discern*

The few other verbs that behave like discernir are: cernir, concernir, hendir

1b. Other radical-changing **-ir** verbs with root vowel **e also** form the present tense by changing **e** → **ie** in all singular forms and the third person plural:

Preferir - ***to prefer***

pref**ie**ro	*I prefer, I do prefer*
pref**ie**res	*you prefer, you do prefer*
Vd. pref**ie**re	*you (formal) prefer, you do prefer*
él/ella/Manolo pref**ie**re	*he/she/Manolo prefer, does prefer*
preferimos	*we prefer, we do prefer*
preferís	*you (pl) prefer, you do prefer*
Vds. pref**ie**ren	*you (formal pl) prefer, you do prefer*
ellos/ellas pref**ie**ren	*they prefer, they do prefer*
Manolo e Isabel pref**ie**ren	*Manolo and Isabel prefer, do prefer*

Some other verbs that behave like **preferir** are:

adherir, advertir, convertir, divertir, herir, mentir, referir, sentir, sugerir, transferir

However, the important difference between verbs of type 1a and 1b is that those like preferir (1b) follow the **e** → **ie** radical change in the present tense, but they follow the **e** → **i** radical change in some **other** tenses and forms (eg the preterite, the gerund).

2. Some radical-changing **-ir** verbs with root vowel **e** form the present tense by changing **e** → **i** in all singular forms and the third person plural:

Pedir - ***to request***

p**i**do	*I request, I do request*
p**i**des	*you request, you do request*
Vd. p**i**de	*you (formal) request, you do request*
él/ella/Manolo p**i**de	*he/she/Manolo requests, does request*
pedimos	*we request, we do request*
pedís	*you (pl) request, you do request*
Vds. p**i**den	*you (formal pl) request, you do request*
ellos/ellas p**i**den	*they request, they do request*
Manolo e Isabel p**i**den	*Manolo and Isabel request, do request*

Other common verbs that behave like **pedir** are:

competir, concebir, conseguir*, consentir, corregir*, despedir, elegir*, gemir, impedir, perseguir*, regir*, repetir, seguir*, servir, vestir

* Verbs marked with an asterisk behave like **pedir** but, in addition, are subject to the rules (nos. 3 or 5, page 66) on spelling changes. Verbs affected are those ending in **-gir** and **-guir**, and the only form changed is the first person singular (eg regir → **rij**o, seguir → **sig**o).

3. Radical-changing **-ir** verbs with root vowel **o** form the present tense by changing **o** → **ue** in all singular forms and the third person plural:

Dormir - ***to sleep***

d**ue**rmo	*I sleep, I do sleep*
d**ue**rmes	*you sleep, you do sleep*
Vd. d**ue**rme	*you (formal) sleep, you do sleep*
él/ella/Manolo d**ue**rme	*he/she/Manolo sleeps, does sleep*
dormimos	*we sleep, we do sleep*
dormís	*you (pl) sleep, you do sleep*
Vds. d**ue**rmen	*you (formal pl) sleep, you do sleep*
ellos/ellas d**ue**rmen	*they sleep, they do sleep*
Manolo e Isabel d**ue**rmen	*Manolo and Isabel sleep, do sleep*

The only other verb like **dormir** is **morir**.
Both verbs are again unusual in that they follow the **o** → **ue** radical change in the present tense, but they follow the **o** → **u** in some other tenses (eg the preterite).

(c) Present Tense of Irregular -ir Verbs

1. Verbs ending in **-ucir** create a first person singular form which ends in **-uzco**. They are otherwise regular in the present tense.

Example: producir → prod**uzco** *I produce, I do produce*

Other common verbs that behave like **producir** are:

aducir, conducir, deducir, introducir, lucir, reducir, seducir, traducir

(Note that verbs ending in **-ducir** undergo further spelling changes in the preterite.)

2. A few very common verbs are sufficiently irregular to be given in full. The present tense conjugations of **decir, ir, oír, reír (sonreír), salir** and **venir** can be found in the Verb Table, pages 103-107.

Present Tense of Reflexive Verbs

Reflexive verbs have **se** added on to the end of the infinitive: levantar**se**, vestir**se**, etc. The extra pronoun often shows that the object *(the person receiving the action of the verb)* is the same person as the subject *(the person performing the action of the verb).* The reflexive pronoun is put between the subject pronoun (when there is one) and the verb, which follows its usual pattern:

Example:	**Me** lavo	*I wash **(myself)***
	Vd. **se** afeita	*You shave **(yourself)***

1. Reflexive verbs are often used when referring to a part of the body (and as a result replace the English possessive adjective):
   Example: **Me** peino el pelo — *I comb **my** hair*

2. Remember to use the correct form of the reflexive pronoun for the person of the verb you are using. There are 6 of them: **me, te, se, nos, os, se**
   Example: (yo) **me**, (tú) **te**, (Vd./él/ella/Manolo) **se**,
   (nosotros) **nos**, (vosostros) **os**, (Vds./ellos/ellas/los niños) **se**

3. When the reflexive verb is used in its infinitive form, remember that the reflexive pronoun has to agree with the subject of the verb.
   Example: Debo levantar**me** temprano mañana por la mañana
   I must get up early tomorrow morning
   Vamos a acostar**nos** a las diez y media
   We are going to go to bed at 10.30

Levantarse - *to get up*

me levant**o**	*I get up, I do get up*
te levant**as**	*you get up, you do get up*
Vd. **se** levant**a**	*you (formal) get up, you do get up*
él/ella/Manolo **se** levant**a**	*he/she/Manolo gets up, does get up*
nos levant**amos**	*we get up, we do get up*
os levant**áis**	*you (pl) get up, you do get up*
Vds. **se** levant**an**	*you (formal pl) get up, you do get up*
ellos/ellas **se** levant**an**	*they get up, they do get up*
Manolo e Isabel **se** levant**an**	*Manolo and Isabel get up, do get up*

Many verbs from all three conjugations exist in Spanish in both normal and reflexive forms with different meanings. For example, **despertar** means *to wake (someone) up* as in *"Ann woke up her son"*; **despertarse** means *to wake up (oneself)* as in *"she woke up in the middle of the night"*.

Some of the most commonly used reflexive verbs are:

aburrirse	*to be bored*	asustarse	*to be frightened*
acercarse a	*to approach*	bañarse	*to bathe*
acostarse*	*to go to bed*	cansarse	*to get tired*
afeitarse	*to shave*	convertirse* en	*to turn into*
alegrarse	*to be glad*	despertarse*	*to wake up*
alejarse de	*to move away from*	desvestirse*	*to undress*
apresurarse	*to hurry*	detenerse*	*to stop*

divertirse*	*to have fun*	marcharse	*to go away*
dormirse*	*to fall asleep*	pararse	*to stop*
ducharse	*to take a shower*	pasearse	*to go for a stroll*
enamorarse	*to fall in love*	peinarse	*to comb one's hair*
enojarse	*to get angry*	pelearse con	*to quarrel with*
hacerse	*to become*	ponerse	*to put on*
hacerse daño/mal	*to hurt oneself*	preocuparse	*to be worried*
interesarse en/por	*to take an interest in*	quitarse	*to take off*
irse	*to go off/away*	sentarse*	*to sit down*
lavarse	*to wash oneself*	sentirse*	*to feel*
llamarse	*to be called*	vestirse*	*to get dressed*
maquillarse	*to put on make-up*		

* Verbs marked with an asterisk are radical-changing. Compounds of irregular verbs such as **hacer, poner, tener,** etc are irregular in the same way.

Special Constructions Using The Present Tense

1. **desde hace** - ***for, since*** uses a present tense in Spanish to convey a meaning which, in English, seems to require a perfect tense. If the action started in the past but is still continuing, then you must use a present tense with **desde hace**:
   Example: Estudio el español **desde hace** tres años
   I have been studying Spanish ***for*** *three years* (and am still doing so)
   Vive en Malvern **desde hace** mucho tiempo
   He has been living in Malvern ***for*** *a long time* (and still does)

2. **acabar de** - ***to have just***
   The present tense of **acabar + de** + infinitive conveys the meaning of *to have just done something.*
   Example: **Acabo de** comer una manzana — *I have just eaten an apple*
   Ella acaba de llegar — *She has just arrived*

3. **soler** - ***to be accustomed to***
   The present tense of soler (radical-changing) + infinitive conveys the meaning of *to be accustomed to, to be wont to, to do something frequently and regularly.*
   Example: **Solemos beber** una taza de té antes de acostarnos
   We ***are accustomed to drinking*** *a cup of tea before going to bed*
   Suele hacer sus deberes en la mesa del comedor
   He ***usually*** *does his homework on the dining-room table*

4. **volver a** - ***to do something again*** conveys the meaning of repeated action.
   Example: **Vuelves a** bañarte — *You take* ***another*** *bath*
   Volvemos a empezar el juego — *We start the game* ***again***

5. **estar a punto de** - ***to be about to*** conveys the meaning of immediate future.
   Example: **Estoy a punto** de salir — ***I am just about to*** *go out*
   Ella está a punto de decidirse — ***She's about to*** *make up her mind* (= on the point of deciding)

THE PROGRESSIVE OR CONTINUOUS PRESENT TENSE (LA FORMA PROGRESIVA)

Formation of the Gerund

The Spanish gerund corresponds roughly to the English present participle, that is the form of the verb which ends *-ing*: *work**ing**, laugh**ing**, answer**ing***.

To form the gerund: remove the **-ar** ending from the infinitive, and add **-ando**
or remove the **-er/-ir** ending from the infinitive, and add **–iendo**

Example: **-ar** verbs - trabaj**ar** → trabaj**ando**
-er verbs - corr**er** → corr**iendo**
-ir verbs - part**ir** → part**iendo**

Exceptions:

1. As in spelling rule 9 on page 66, **-er** and **-ir** verbs ending in two vowels change the **-i-** in **-iendo** to **-y-**, **-yendo**:
   Example: tr**aer** → tra**yendo** infl**uir** → influ**yendo**

2. Radical-changing **-ir** verbs that behave like **preferir** (1b, page 70) and **pedir** (2, page 71) change **e** → **i** in their root when forming the gerund:
   Example: sentir → s**intiendo** repetir → repi**tiendo**

3. There are a few irregular gerunds (mostly from irregular -ir verbs):

decir → **diciendo**	dormir → **durmiendo**	ir → **yendo**
morir → **muriendo**	oír → **oyendo**	poder → **pudiendo**
reír → **riendo**	sonreír → **sonriendo**	venir → **viniendo**

Formation of the Continuous Present

The continuous present in English is that form of the present created with the verb *to be* plus the present participle: *I am shouting, we are building*, etc. To form the continuous present in Spanish, **estar**, conjugated in the normal way, is combined with the gerund:
Example: **Estoy cultivando** el jardín ***I'm working on*** *the garden*
Están siguiendo el camino ***They are following*** *the path*

The Spanish continuous present can **only** refer to something going on at the time of utterance. It cannot refer to future time as in English phrases such as *I'm taking next week off.*

Other Uses of the Gerund

1. The gerund is invariable - that is, it does not change its spelling:
   Example: **Viendo** que él dormía, ella salió
   Seeing *that he was asleep, she went out*
   Se han marchado, **dejando** a María sola en casa
   They have gone off, ***leaving*** *María alone at home*

2. Remember that pronouns are attached to the end of the gerund:
   Example: Escribió una carta pidiéndo**melo** *He wrote a letter asking* ***me for it***

3. Various other verbs besides **estar**, such as **ir, venir, andar** and **seguir** can be combined with the gerund:

   Example: **Iba** adelgazando cada vez más
   He was growing thinner and thinner
   Andas pidiendo dinero a todo el mundo
   You go around asking everybody for money
   Siguieron hablando en voz baja
   They continued/carried on talking in a low voice

4. The gerund is used to show method of motion after verbs such as **entrar, salir, bajar, subir** and **atravesar:**

   Example: Ella entró/salió **corriendo** *She ran in/out*
   Atravesé el aula **tambaleando** *I staggered across the classroom*

5. Spanish has a different form for the present participle, **-ar** → **-ante**, **-er** and **-ir** → **-ente** or **-iente**, but most verbs **do not** create this form at all. When they do, the present participle is typically used as an adjective:

   Example: una mujer **sonriente** *a smiling woman*
   unos futbolistas **principiantes** *novice footballers*

6. Notice that where we would use a present participle in English, it is often better to use a relative clause in Spanish:

   Example: Había un grupo de niños **que jugaba** en el bosque
   There was a group of children playing in the wood

The Preterite Tense (El Pretérito Indefinido)

Use of the Preterite

This is the standard past tense used in conversation, letters, newspapers, the narrative sections of stories and novels and history books to describe:

- a completed action in the past
- a series of completed events in a story
- an action in the past which happened on one occasion only

   Example: Ella **subió** al tercer piso *She went up to the third floor*
   Él **murió** en 1930 *He died in 1930*
   Ellos **salieron** de la casa, **atravesaron** la calle y **entraron** en la tienda
   They left the house, crossed the street and went into the shop

Formation of the Preterite - Regular Verbs

To form the preterite of any regular **-ar** verb, you take the final **-ar** away from the infinitive and add the endings: **-é, -aste, -ó, -amos, -asteis, -aron**

Trabajar - *to work*

trabaj**é**	*I worked*	trabaj**amos**	*we worked*
trabaj**aste**	*you worked*	trabaj**asteis**	*you (pl) worked*
Vd. trabaj**ó**	*you (formal) worked*	Vds. trabaj**aron**	*you (formal pl) worked*
él/ella trabaj**ó**	*he/she worked*	ellos/ellas trabaj**aron**	*they worked*
Manolo trabaj**ó**	*Manolo worked*	Manolo e Isabel trabaj**aron**	*M. and I. worked*

Some otherwise regular **-ar** verbs undergo spelling changes in the first person singular of the preterite:
verbs ending in **-car** (buscar → bus**qué**) verbs ending in **-gar** (llegar → lle**gué**)
verbs ending in **-guar** (averiguar → averi**güé**) verbs ending in **-zar** (cazar → ca**cé**)
(See rules 2, 4, 6 and 8 on page 66.)

To form the preterite of any regular **-er** or **-ir** verb, you take the final **-er** or **-ir** away from the infinitive and add the endings: **-í, -iste, -ió, -imos, -isteis, -ieron**

Vender - ***to sell***

vend**í**	*I sold*	vend**imos**	*we sold*
vend**iste**	*you sold*	vend**isteis**	*you (pl) sold*
Vd. vend**ió**	*you (formal) sold*	Vds. vend**ieron**	*you (formal pl) sold*
él/ella vend**ió**	*he/she sold*	ellos/ellas vend**ieron**	*they sold*
Manolo vend**ió**	*Manolo sold*	Manolo e Isabel vend**ieron**	*Manolo and Isabel sold*

Abrir - ***to open***

abr**í**	*I opened*	abr**imos**	*we opened*
abr**iste**	*you opened*	abr**isteis**	*you (pl)opened*
Vd. abr**ió**	*you (formal) opened*	Vds. abr**ieron**	*you (formal pl) opened*
él/ella abr**ió**	*he/she opened*	ellos/ellas abr**ieron**	*they opened*
Manolo abr**ió**	*Manolo opened*	Manolo e Isabel abr**ieron**	*M. and I. opened*

Some otherwise regular **-er** and **-ir** verbs undergo spelling changes in the third person singular and plural: verbs in **-aer, -eer, -oer, -oír, uir** (eg leer → le**yó**, le**yeron**; roer → ro**yó**, ro**yeron**; construir → constru**yó**, constru**yeron**) (rule 9, page 66). The same rule also applies to verbs like **caer, traer**, etc.

Radical-changing Verbs

All radical-changing **-ar** verbs (eg **pensar, mostrar,** also **jugar**) behave like entirely regular **-ar** verbs in forming the preterite. Note that the appropriate rule again applies when they have endings that fall under the spelling changes rules (page 66), as with:
negar, comenzar, trocar, colgar and **almorzar**

Likewise, all radical-changing **-er** verbs (eg **perder, volver**) behave like entirely regular **-er** verbs in forming the preterite. Furthermore, the few radical-changing **-ir** verbs like **discernir** (Type 1a) also behave like regular **-ir** verbs in the preterite.

However, radical-changing **-ir** verbs like **preferir** (type 1b), **pedir** (type 2) and **dormir** (type 3) **do** make changes in the preterite in the third person singular and plural.
See pages 70-71.

Type 1b **and** type 2 verbs behave like **seguir -** *to follow*:

seguí	*I followed*	seguimos	*we followed*
seguiste	*you followed*	seguisteis	*you (pl) followed*
Vd. s**i**guió	*you (formal) followed*	Vds. s**i**guieron	*you (formal pl) followed*
él/ella s**i**guió	*he/she followed*	ellos/ellas s**i**guieron	*they followed*
Manolo s**i**guió	*Manolo followed*	Manolo e Isabel s**i**guieron	*M. and I. followed*

Dormir and **morir** (type 3) similarly form the preterite in this way:
dormí, dormiste, d**u**rmió dormimos, dormisteis, d**u**rmieron

Irregular Verbs

The preterite of irregular **-ar** verbs **dar** and **estar** is given in the Verb Table.
The otherwise regular verb **andar** forms the preterite irregularly (see Verb Table).

The preterite of irregular **-er** verbs **caber, haber, hacer, poder, poner, querer, saber, satisfacer, ser, tener** and **ver** is given in the Verb Table, pages 103-107.

All **-ir** verbs ending in **-ducir** form the preterite irregularly. These verbs behave like **producir** - *to produce*

produ**je**	*I produced*	produ**jimos**	*we produced*
produ**jiste**	*you produced*	produ**jisteis**	*you (pl) produced*
Vd. produ**jo**	*you (formal) produced*	Vds. produ**jeron**	*you (formal pl) produced*
él/ella produ**jo**	*he/she produced*	ellos/ellas produ**jeron**	*they produced*
Manolo produ**jo**	*Manolo produced*	M. e Isabel produ**jeron**	*M. and I. produced*

The preterite of irregular **-ir** verbs **decir, ir, oír, reír (sonreír), salir** and **venir** is given in the Verb Table.

THE IMPERFECT TENSE (EL PRETÉRITO IMPERFECTO)

Use of the Imperfect

This is the tense which translates the English *was -ing,* or *used to* ... In Spanish it is used:

1. for describing continuing states, events or feelings in the past:
   Example: Las ventanas **hacían** ruido, **nevaba** y el niño **tenía** miedo
   *The windows were **rattling**, **it was snowing** and the boy **was afraid***

2. for talking or writing about repeated actions in the past:
   Example: Cada mañana él **salía** de la casa a las ocho
   *He **left/used to leave** the house at eight o'clock every morning*

3. for referring to incomplete actions in the past - actions interrupted by another action:
   Example: Mientras yo **lavaba** los platos sonó el teléfono
   *While **I was doing** the dishes, the telephone rang*

   The subject pronoun **yo** often appears in the imperfect tense to help distinguish between first and third person singular forms.

4. for reported speech:
   Example: - Estoy muy descontenta
   "I am very unhappy"
   becomes Ella dijo que estaba muy descontenta
   She said that she was very unhappy

Formation of the Imperfect Tense

To form the imperfect of all **-ar** verbs, you take the final **-ar** away from the infinitive and add the endings: **-aba, -abas, -aba, -ábamos, -abais, -aban**

Trabajar - ***to work***

yo trabaj**aba**	*I was working, I used to work, I worked*
trabaj**abas**	*you were working, you used to work, you worked*
Vd. trabaj**aba**	*you (formal) were working, you used to work, you worked*
él/ella/Manolo trabaj**aba**	*he/she/Manolo was working, used to work, worked*
trabaj**ábamos**	*we were working, we used to work, we worked*
trabaj**abais**	*you (pl) were working, you used to work, you worked*
Vds. trabaj**aban**	*you (formal pl) were working, you used to work, you worked*
ellos/ellas trabaj**aban**	*they were working, they used to work, they worked*
Manolo e Isabel trabaj**aban**	*Manolo and Isabel were working, used to work, worked*

To form the imperfect of all **-er** and **-ir** verbs, you take the final **-er** or **-ir** away from the infinitive and add the endings: **-ía, -ías, -ía, -íamos, -íais, -ían**

Vender - ***to sell***

yo vend**ía**	*I was selling, I used to sell, I sold*
vend**ías**	*you were selling, you used to sell, you sold*
Vd. vend**ía**	*you (formal) were selling, you used to sell, you sold*
él/ella/Manolo vend**ía**	*he/she/Manolo was selling, used to sell, sold*
vend**íamos**	*we were selling, we used to sell, we sold*
vend**íais**	*you (pl)were selling, you used to sell, you sold*
Vds. vend**ían**	*you (formal pl) were selling, you used to sell, you sold*
ellos/ellas vend**ían**	*they were selling, they used to sell, they sold*
Manolo e Isabel vend**ían**	*Manolo and Isabel were selling, used to sell, sold*

Abrir - ***to open***

yo abr**ía**	*I was opening, I used to open, I opened*
abr**ías**	*you were opening, you used to open, you opened*
Vd. abr**ía**	*you (formal) were opening, you used to open, you opened*
él/ella/Manolo abr**ía**	*he/she/Manolo was opening, used to open, opened*
abr**íamos**	*we were opening, we used to open, we opened*
abr**íais**	*you (pl)were opening, you used to open, you opened*
Vds. abr**ían**	*you (formal pl) were opening, you used to open, you opened*
ellos/ellas abr**ían**	*they were opening, they used to open, they opened*
Manolo e Isabel abr**ían**	*Manolo and Isabel were opening, used to open, opened*

No radical-changing verbs make any changes in the imperfect. The only irregular verbs in this tense are **ser**, **ver** and **ir**. **Ver** retains the **-e-** of its root but is otherwise regular (v**eía**, v**eías**, etc); all three verbs appear in the Verb Table, pages 103-107.

THE PERFECT TENSE (EL PRETÉRITO PERFECTO)

Use of the Perfect Tense

This tense translates the English *I **have** sneezed, you **have** gone, he **has** travelled*, etc. It usually refers to an action in the past still connected to the present in some way:

- because it occurred a very short time ago,
- because the period of time in which it occurred runs up to the present, or
- because it has some bearing on the present.

Example:	El reloj **ha dado** las ocho	*The clock **has** (just) **struck** eight*
	La **he visitado** dos veces este año	***I have visited** her twice this year (so far)*
	Alguien **ha comido** mi sopa	*Someone **has eaten** my soup*

Formation of the Perfect Tense

The perfect tense is made up of two parts: the auxiliary verb **haber** + the past participle. **Haber** always functions as an auxiliary verb; it is irregular and it appears in the Verb Table. Spanish uses a different verb, **tener**, for the normal meanings of *to have*:

Example:	**Tengo** cien euros	***I have** a hundred euros*
	Tenemos muchos parientes	***We have** a lot of relatives*

Formation of the Past Participle

In English, past participles often end in **-en, -ed** or **-t** (*hidd**en**, look**ed**, bough**t***). In Spanish, to form the past participles of **-ar** verbs remove the **-ar** ending and add **-ado**; to form the past participles of **-er** and **-ir** verbs, remove either ending and add **-ido**. Thus:

trabajar → trabajado **vender → vendido** **partir → partido**

There are no irregular past participles of **-ar** verbs; however, there are quite a few irregular past participles of **-er** and **-ir** verbs; several (eg **abrir**) are entirely regular except for the formation of their past participle. Here are some common examples:

caer → caído*	roer → roído*	abrir → abierto	ir → ido
creer → creído*	romper → roto	cubrir → cubierto	morir → muerto
hacer → hecho	satisfacer → satisfecho	decir → dicho	oír → oído*
leer → leído*	traer → traído*	escribir → escrito	pudrir → podrido
poner → puesto	ver → visto	freír → frito	reír → reído*
proveer → provisto	volver → vuelto	imprimir → impreso	sonreír → sonreído*

(*= *added accent*)

The perfect tense itself has no unusual features: it is **always** formed with the present tense of **haber** (an irregular verb) plus the past participle of the verb (either formed regularly or irregularly). **Note that the past participle never agrees with the subject in any way.**

he trabajado	he vendido	he abierto
has trabajado	has vendido	has abierto
Vd. ha trabajado	Vd. ha vendido	Vd. abierto
él/ella ha trabajado	él/ella ha vendido	él/ella ha abierto
Manolo ha trabajado	Manolo ha vendido	Manolo ha abierto
hemos trabajado	hemos vendido	hemos abierto
habéis trabajado	habéis vendido	habéis abierto
Vds. han trabajado	Vds. han vendido	Vds. han abierto
ellos/ellas han trabajado	ellos/ellas han vendido	ellos/ellas han abierto
M. e I. han trabajado	M. e I. han vendido	M. e I. han abierto

THE PLUPERFECT TENSE (EL PRETÉRITO PLUSCUAMPERFECTO)

Use of the Pluperfect Tense

This tense translates the English *I **had** given, we **had** been thinking, they **had** played, etc.*

1. It is used to talk or write about events in the past which had happened before other past events took place:
   Example: Me llamó por teléfono porque **había perdido** la dirección
   *He called me on the phone because **he had lost** the address*

2. It is also used to report what other people had said (reported speech)
   Example: - Llegué al colegio a las nueve menos cuarto
   "I got to school at a quarter to nine"
   becomes, in reported speech:
   Ella dijo que **había llegado** al instituto a las nueve menos cuarto
   *She said that **she had got to** school at a quarter to nine*

Formation of the Pluperfect Tense

The pluperfect tense is formed in the same way as the perfect tense, except that the Imperfect tense of the auxiliary **haber** is used in place of the present tense.
All other rules concerning the perfect tense apply in exactly the same way. (See page 79)

Decir - ***to say***

yo	había dicho	*I had said*
	habías dicho	*you had said*
Vd.	había dicho	*you (formal) had said*
él/ella	había dicho	*he/she had said*
Manolo	había dicho	*Manolo had said*
	habíamos dicho	*we had said*
	habíais dicho	*you (pl) had said*
Vds.	habían dicho	*you (formal pl) had said*
ellos/ellas	habían dicho	*they had said*
Manolo e Isabel	habían dicho	*Manolo and Isabel had said*

THE FUTURE TENSE (EL FUTURO)

Use of the Future Tense

The future tense in Spanish is used:
- to talk and write about things which definitely **will** happen
- to refer to events which will take place at some time in the future rather than in the short term

Remember that there are more forms of the future in English than there are in Spanish. *He will see her* and *He will be seeing her* are both translated as **Él la verá**.

If you wish to talk or write about something which will happen in the fairly near future, you can use the present tense: ¿Vuelves pronto? *Are you coming back soon?*

Alternatively, you can create a construction with the present tense of **ir + a + the infinitive** like the English: *He **is going to play** football on Saturday*:

Example:	¿**Vas a** part**ir** pronto?	***Are you going to/Will you** leave soon?*
	Van a lleg**ar** tarde	*They **will/are going to** arrive late*

Formation of the Future Tense

To form the future tense of all regular **-ar**, **-er** and **-ir** verbs, just add the future endings **-é, -ás, -á, -emos, -éis, -án** on to the infinitive. (Don't remove anything!)

Trabajar - *to work*

trabajar**é**	*I shall work, I shall be working*
trabajar**ás**	*you will work, you will be working*
Vd. trabajar**á**	*you (formal) will work, you will be working*
él/ella/Manolo trabajar**á**	*he/she/Manolo will work, will be working*
trabajar**emos**	*we shall work, we shall be working*
trabajar**éis**	*you (pl) will work, you will be working*
Vds. trabajar**án**	*you (formal plural) will work, you will be working*
ellos/ellas trabajar**án**	*they will work, they will be working*
Manolo e Isabel trabajar**án**	*Manolo and Isabel will work, will be working*

In exactly the same way, vender → vender**é**, vender**ás**, etc

Irregular Future Tenses

There are some commonly used **-er** and **-ir** verbs which do not form the future directly from the infinitive; instead, they have an irregular stem and these have to be learned individually. There are **no** irregular **-ar** verbs.
Once you know the stem form, you can add the endings in the normal way:

Infinitive	**Future**
caber	→ cabré, cabrás, cabrá, cabremos, cabréis, cabrán
decir	→ diré, dirás, dirá, diremos, diréis, dirán
haber	→ habré, habrás, habrá, habremos, habréis, habrán
hacer	→ haré, harás, hará, haremos, haréis, harán
poder	→ podré, podrás, podrá, podremos, podréis, podrán
poner	→ pondré, pondrás, pondrá, pondremos, pondréis, pondrán
querer	→ querré, querrás, querrá, querremos, querréis, querrán
saber	→ sabré, sabrás, sabrá, sabremos, sabréis, sabrán
salir	→ saldré, saldrás, saldrá, saldremos, saldréis, saldrán
tener	→ tendré, tendrás, tendrá, tendremos, tendréis, tendrán
valer	→ valdré, valdrás, valdrá, valdremos, valdréis, valdrán
venir	→ vendré, vendrás, vendrá, vendremos, vendréis, vendrán

Verbs like **oír** → oiré and **reír** → reiré drop the accent which appears on the infinitive.

The Conditional Tense (El Potencial Simple)

Use of the Conditional Tense

This is the tense used to talk or write about things which you **would** do.
It is how you express the idea of conditions or unfulfilled statements about the future.

Example: Me **gustaría** viajar al Japón pero no tengo bastante dinero
I would like to travel to Japan but I haven't (got) enough money

It is how you talk or write about something anticipated in the future from a point in the past.

Example: Ella insistió en que lo **terminaría** esa noche
*She insisted that she **would finish** it that night*

It is also how you express assumptions or approximations referring to the past.

Example: **Estaría** todavía soltero cuando lo conocí por primera vez
*He **must** still **have been** single when I first met him*
Ayer Vd. **escribiría** unas diez páginas
*Yesterday **you must have written** about ten pages*

Formation of the Conditional

The conditional tense is something of a "mongrel" in its formation! It is a Future crossed with the Imperfect - you combine the **stem** (regular or irregular) of the Future tense with the **endings** of the Imperfect tense of **-er** and **-ir** verbs: **ía, ías, ía, íamos, íais, ían**

trabajar	→ trabajar**ía**	poner	→ pondr**ía**
vender	→ vender**ía**	querer	→ querr**ía**
abrir	→ abrir**ía**	tener	→ tendr**ía**
hacer	→ har**ía**	decir	→ dir**ía**
poder	→ podr**ía**	venir	→ vendr**ía**

As with the future tense, verbs like oír → oir**ía** drop the accent on the infinitive.

As with the imperfect, if the context does not make it clear, the subject pronoun **yo** is used to differentiate the first person singular form from the third person singular form.

The Passive (La Voz Pasiva)

Use of the Passive

The passive is used when the subject of the verb is also the recipient of the action of the verb:

Example:	**contrast**	**Seguimos** a los niños	
		We follow the children	(active)
	with	**Somos seguidos por** los niños	
		We are being followed by the children	(passive)

Formation of the Passive

To form the passive you use **ser + the past participle** which **must** agree with the subject:

Example: La iglesia fue **diseñada** por un arquitecto famoso
The church was designed by a famous architect

All tenses of the passive can be made up by using the appropriate tense of **ser** plus the past participle of the verb to be made passive:

Example:	Present:	ella es hallad**a**	*she is found*
	Future:	él será hallad**o**	*he will be found*
	Imperfect:	ellos eran hallad**os**	*they (m) used to be found*
	Preterite:	ellas fueron hallad**as**	*they (f) were found*

Remember! The past participle agrees in gender and number with the subject!

Avoidance of the Passive

The passive is avoided as far as possible by using one of the following alternatives:

1. By using the impersonal **se** construction (which is like a reflexive) in the third person singular or plural:

Example:	Eso no **se** hace aquí	*That is not done here*
	Se oían algunos ruidos	*Some sounds were heard*

   Although very common,the impersonal **se** construction cannot be used with an agent introduced by **por**:

   Example: Algunos ruidos **fueron oídos por** los perros (passive)
   *Some sounds **were heard by** the dogs*

2. By using the impersonal third person plural construction *"They ... /People ..."*:

Example:	Le hicieron muchas preguntas	*"They" asked him a lot of questions*
		He was asked a lot of questions
	Dicen que el pozo es profundo	*People say the well is deep*
		It is said that the well is deep

3. By turning the sentence round, and thus making the verb active:

Example:	Él fue detenido por la policía	*He was arrested by the police*
becomes	La policía lo detuvo	*The police arrested him*

Although not a true passive use, the other verb *to be* **estar**, can also be combined with the past participle.
When it is used with **estar,** in this way, the past participle is really functioning as an adjective and it therefore agrees with the noun it qualifies:

Example:	La ventana **está cerrada**	*The window **is closed***
	Ella **estaba aburrida**	*She **was bored***
	El estadio **estará abierto** a partir de las nueve	
	*The stadium **will be open** from 9 o'clock*	

THE PRESENT SUBJUNCTIVE (EL SUBJUNTIVO PRESENTE)

All the tenses treated so far are known as **Indicatives**: they indicate things that *are done, were done, will be done,* etc. The **Subjunctive** is different: it refers, for instance, to things that one *wishes, hopes* or *orders* to be done (but have not yet been done), to things one is uncertain about, or to things in the future that may - or may not - happen.

Formation of the Present Subjunctive

In terms of its manner of formation, the present subjunctive can usefully be thought of as the "reverse" of the present indicative.

1. Most **-ar** verbs form the present subjunctive by taking the first person singular of the present indicative tense, removing the **-o**, and adding the present indicative endings of regular **-er** verbs, except in the first person singular.

Trabajar - *to work* trabajo → trabaj- → trabaj**e**

trabaj**e**	*I may work*
trabaj**es**	*you may work*
Vd. trabaj**e**	*you (formal) may work*
él/ella/Manolo trabaj**e**	*he/she/Manolo may work*
trabaj**emos**	*we may work*
trabaj**éis**	*you (pl) may work*
Vds. trabaj**en**	*you (formal pl) may work*
ellos/ellas trabaj**en**	*they may work*
Manolo e Isabel trabaj**en**	*Manolo and Isabel may work*

The rules on spelling changes for otherwise regular verbs again apply. See page 66. Thus verbs like buscar → bus**que**, bus**ques**, etc; pagar → pa**gue**, pa**gues**, etc; averiguar → averig**üe**, averig**ües**, etc; lanzar → lan**ce**, lan**ces**, etc

2. All regular radical-changing **-ar** verbs (ie those with **-e-**, **-o-** and **-u-** in their root) form the present subjunctive by following the complete root-change pattern in their present indicative conjugation, removing the present indicative ending, and adding the **-er** present indicative ending, except in the first person singular.

Mostrar - *to show*

m**ue**stro → m**ue**str- → m**ue**str**e** **but** m**o**stramos → m**o**str- → m**o**str**emos**

muestr**e**	*I may show*
muestr**es**	*you may show*
Vd. muestr**e**	*you (formal) may show*
él/ella/Manolo muestr**e**	*he/she/Manolo may show*
mostr**emos**	*we may show*
mostr**éis**	*you (pl) may show*
Vds. muestr**en**	*you (formal pl) may show*
ellos/ellas muestr**en**	*they may show*
Manolo e Isabel muestr**en**	*Manolo and Isabel may show*

The rules on spelling (page 66) also apply to radical-changing verbs: thus, for instance: comenzar → comien**ce**, comen**cemos,** etc colgar → cuel**gue**, col**guemos**, etc

3. The present subjunctive of irregular **-ar** verbs is given in the Verb Table.

4. Most **-er** verbs form the present subjunctive by taking the first person singular of the present indicative tense, removing the **-o**, and adding the present indicative endings of regular **-ar** verbs, except in the first person singular.

Vender - ***to sell*** vendo → vend- → vend**a**

vend**a**	*I may sell*
vend**as**	*you may sell*
Vd. vend**a**	*you (formal) may sell*
él/ella/Manolo vend**a**	*he/she/Manolo may sell*
vend**amos**	*we may sell*
vend**áis**	*you (pl) may sell*
Vds. vend**an**	*you (formal pl) may sell*
ellos/ellas vend**an**	*they may sell*
Manolo e Isabel vend**an**	*Manolo and Isabel may sell*

The rules on spelling changes (page 66) for otherwise regular verbs again apply.
Thus verbs like mecer → me**za**, me**zas,** etc; and coger → co**ja**, co**jas,** etc

5. All regular radical-changing **-er** verbs (i.e. those with **-e-** and **-o-** in their root) form the present subjunctive by following the complete root-change pattern throughout their present indicative conjugation, removing the present indicative ending, and adding the present indicative ending of regular **-ar** verbs, except in the first person singular.

Perder - ***to lose***

pierdo → pierd- → pierd**a**	**but** perdemos → perd- → perd**amos**
pierd**a**	*I may lose*
pierd**as**	*you may lose*
Vd. pierd**a**	*you (formal) may lose*
él/ella/Manolo pierd**a**	*he/she/Manolo may lose*
perd**amos**	*we may lose*
perd**áis**	*you (pl) may lose*
Vds. pierd**an**	*you (formal pl) may lose*
ellos/ellas pierd**an**	*they may lose*
Manolo e Isabel pierd**an**	*Manolo and Isabel may lose*

The rules on spelling (page 66) also apply to radical-changing verbs:
Example: torcer → tuer**za**, tor**zamos**, etc

6. The standard rules on present subjunctive formation apply **also** to **-er** verbs that form their first person singular present indicative irregularly. This means that verbs with infinitives in **-acer, -ecer, -ocer** with a first person singular present indicative form ending in **-zco** create the present subjunctive with **-azca**, **ezca**,**-ozca**.
Example: parecer → par**ezca**, par**ezcas**, par**ezca**, par**ezcamos**, par**ezcáis**, par**ezcan**

This rule also applies to:
(a) verbs like caer, traer → ca**iga**, ca**igas**, ca**iga**, ca**igamos**, ca**igáis**, ca**igan**
(b) certain irregular verbs like caber, hacer, poner, satisfacer, tener and valer
Example: caber → quepo → quep**a** tener → tengo → teng**a**

The present subjunctive of irregular **-er** verbs is given in the Verb Table (pages 103-107).

7. Most **-ir** verbs (exactly like most **-er** verbs) form the present subjunctive by taking the first person singular of the present indicative tense, removing the **-o**, and adding the present indicative endings of regular **-ar** verbs, except in the first person singular.

Abrir - ***to open*** abro → abr- → abr**a**

abr**a**	*I may open*
abr**as**	*you may open*
Vd. abr**a**	*you (formal) may open*
él/ella/Manolo abr**a**	*he/she/Manolo may open*
abr**amos**	*we may open*
abr**áis**	*you (pl) may open*
Vds. abr**an**	*you (formal pl) may open*
ellos/ellas abr**an**	*they may open*
Manolo e Isabel abr**an**	*Manolo and Isabel may open*

The rules on spelling changes for otherwise regular verbs again apply. (See page 66)

Thus verbs like		
	esparcir → espar**za**, espar**zas**	fingir → fin**ja**, fin**jas**
	distinguir → distin**ga**, distin**gas**	delinquir → delin**ca**, delin**cas**
	concluir → conclu**ya**, conclu**yas**	

8a. Radical-changing **-ir** verbs like **discernir** form the present subjunctive by following the complete root-change pattern throughout their present indicative conjugation, removing the present indicative ending, and adding the **-ar** present indicative ending, except in the first person singular.
(In other words, they behave like **-ar** and **-er** radical-changing verbs.)

8b. Radical-changing verbs like **preferir** and **dormir** form the present subjunctive by following the complete root-change pattern throughout their present indicative conjugation, removing the present indicative ending, and adding the **-ar** present indicative ending, except in the first person singular.
In addition the first and second person plural forms undergo a further root change **e** → **i** and **o** → **u**:

Example: sentir - sentimos - s**i**ntamos dormir - dormís - d**u**rmáis

Preferir - ***to prefer***

prefiero → prefier- → prefier**a** **but** preferimos → prefir**amos**

prefier**a**	*I may prefer*
prefier**as**	*you may prefer*
Vd. prefier**a**	*you (formal) may prefer*
él/ella/Manolo prefier**a**	*he/she/Manolo may prefer*
prefir**amos**	*we may prefer*
prefir**áis**	*you (pl) may prefer*
Vds. prefier**an**	*you (formal pl) may prefer*
ellos/ellas prefier**an**	*they may prefer*
Manolo e Isabel prefier**an**	*Manolo and Isabel may prefer*

8c. Radical-changing verbs like **pedir** behave like regular **-ir** verbs, in that they form the present subjunctive by taking the first person singular of the present indicative tense, removing the **-o**, and adding the present indicative endings of regular **-ar** verbs, except in the first person singular. (In other words, the root change **e** → **i** is maintained through **all six** person and number forms of the verb.)

Pedir - ***to request*** pido → pid- → pid**a**

pid**a**	*I may request*
pid**as**	*you may request*
Vd. pid**a**	*you (formal) may request*
él/ella/Manolo pid**a**	*he/she/Manolo may request*
pid**amos**	*we may request*
pid**áis**	*you (pl)may request*
Vds. pid**an**	*you (formal pl) may request*
ellos/ellas pid**an**	*they may request*
Manolo e Isabel pid**an**	*Manolo and Isabel may request*

The rules on spelling changes for otherwise regular verbs again apply. (See page 66)
Thus verbs like corregir → corr**ija**, corr**ijas,** etc; and seguir → **siga**, si**gas,** etc

9. The standard rules on present subjunctive formation apply **also** to **-ir** verbs which form their first person singular present indicative irregularly.

Thus verbs whose infinitive ends in **-ucir** form the present subjunctive as follows:

Example: producir → prod**uzca** prod**uzcas** prod**uzca**
prod**uzcamos** prod**uzcáis** prod**uzcan**

The same rule applies to irregular verbs like **decir, oír, salir** and **venir**:

Example: decir → digo → dig**a**, etc venir → vengo → veng**a**, etc

The present subjunctive of irregular **-ir** verbs is given in the Verb Table, pages 103-107.

Use of the Present Subjunctive

The present subjunctive has a number of different uses.

1. It creates the **positive command forms** for Vd.,Vds. and nosotros: it also creates the **negative commands** for tú, vosotros, nosotros, Vd. and Vds.
See Command Forms on pages 88-89.

2. It is the form of the verb used with a number of conjunctions, most of which refer to an event in the future or an event that is uncertain or which express the idea of purpose. See Conjunctions on pages 27-28.

3. It is used in clauses after verbs that exert influence, verbs of emotion, verbs of subjective opinion and verbs of uncertainty. In all these cases the subject will be different between the main clause and the subordinate clause with the subjunctive.

Example:	Te persuadiré de que lo **hagas**	*I shall persuade you to do it*
	Él se alegra de que **ganemos**	*He is happy that we are winning*
	Es aceptable que otro **venga**	*It is acceptable that someone else comes*
	No creo que **digas** la verdad	*I don't believe that you're telling the truth*

4. It is used in **certain exclamations**, such as
"¡Viva España!" *Long live Spain!* "¡Viva la reina!" *Long live the Queen!*
"¡Que aproveche!" *Bon appétit!/Enjoy your meal!*

COMMAND FORMS (EL IMPERATIVO)

Use of the Command Form

Command forms, also called Imperatives, are used to tell someone to do, or not to do something. There are five command forms for each verb, which correspond to **tú** and **vosotros**, to **Vd.** and **Vds.**, and to **nosotros**.

Remember that you should use the **tú/vosotros** and **Vd./Vds.** forms according to the usual rules for these pronouns. See Pronouns on page 50.
The **nosotros** form is used to translate the English *"Let's (Let **us**) do something"*.

Formation of Commands

Remember that object pronouns are attached to the end of positive imperatives, but occupy their normal position with negative imperatives. See page 53.

1. The **tú** form is created from the second person singular present indicative tense of the verb, from which the final **-s** is removed. This applies to all regular verbs, all radical-changing verbs and most irregular verbs.

Example:	Trabaja mucho	Piénsalo	Vuelve mañana	Pídeselo
	Do lots of work	*Think it over*	*Come back tomorrow*	*Ask him for it*

There are some irregular forms:

hacer → haz	poner → pon	satisfacer → satisfaz	ser → sé	tener → ten
decir → di	ir → ve	salir → sal	venir → ven	

2. The **vosotros** form is created by substituting the final **-r** of the infinitive with **-d**:

Example:	Trabajad mucho	Pensadlo	Volved mañana	Pedídselo
	Do lots of work	*Think it over*	*Come back tomorrow*	*Ask him for it*

There are **no** irregularities in the **vosotros** form itself, but the **-d** is dropped with reflexive verbs: lavad *wash* lavaos *wash yourselves* vestid *dress* vestíos *get dressed*

3. However, the **negative** imperatives for the **tú** and **vosotros** pronouns are created with the corresponding forms of the present subjunctive.

Example:	Trabaja →	No trabaj**es**	Vende →	No vend**as**	Abre →	No abr**as**
	Muestra →	No muestr**es**	Vuelve →	No vuelv**as**	Pide →	No pid**as**
	Da →	No d**es**	Pon →	No pong**as**	Ven →	No veng**as**
and likewise:	Trabajad →	No trabaj**éis**	Volved →	No volv**áis**	Venid →	No veng**áis**

4. The **nosotros** forms - both positive and negative - are created with the first person plural of the present subjunctive.

Example:	Trabaj**emos**	No trabaj**emos**	Volv**amos**	No volv**amos**
	Let's work	*Let's not work*	*Let's go back*	*Let's not go back*
	Sig**amos**	No sig**amos**	Salg**amos**	No salg**amos**
	Let's go on	*Let's not go on*	*Let's go out*	*Let's not go out*

The only irregular form is **ir** → vamos. A common way to express the sense of *Let's ...* is to use **Vamos** + **a** + infinitive: Vamos a cantar *Let's sing* Vamos a ver *Let's see*

5. The **Vd.** and **Vds.** forms - again both positive and negative - are created with the third person singular and third person plural of the present subjunctive.

Example:	Pas**e** Vd.	Tranquilíc**e**se Vd.	D**é**selo Vd.
	Please come in	*Calm down/yourself*	*Give it to him*
	No lo niegu**e** Vd.	No se muev**a** Vd.	No le corrij**a** Vd.
	Don't deny it	*Don't (you) move*	*Don't correct him*
and likewise:	Cáll**ense** Vds.	No lo toqu**en** Vds.	No pid**an** nada
	Be quiet	*Don't touch it*	*Don't ask for anything*

The standard way to answer a telephone in Spanish is:
"¡Diga!" or "¡Dígame!" *Hello* (literally "tell (me)!")

NEGATIVES (LAS FORMAS NEGATIVAS)

Use of Negatives

Negatives are the words put with a verb to change its positive meaning to the reverse; it then says that something will *not/never/no longer* happen.
In Spanish, the basic negative is **no**; other negatives usually have two parts - **no** plus a second part which varies according to meaning.

no	*not*	no ... tampoco	*not either*
no ... nunca	*never*	no ... ninguno (ún, -a, -os, -as)	*no, not one*
no ... jamás	*never*	no ... ni ... ni	*neither ... nor*
no ... nada	*nothing*	no ... más de	*not more than*
no ... nadie	*nobody*	no ... más que	*only*
no ... apenas	*hardly*	no ... ni	*not even*
ya no ...	*not ... any more*	no ... ni siquiera	*not even*

Word order with Negatives

1. The general rule is that in simple tenses the **no** comes before the verb (or the pronoun(s) before the verb) and the second part of the negative, if there is one, follows it:

Example:	**No** veo la televisión	*I don't watch television*
	No veo **nunca** la televisión	*I never watch television*
	No la veo **apenas**	*I scarcely watch it*
	Ya no veo la televisión	*I don't watch television any more*

2. When you use a negative with a compound tense the second part of the negative, if there is one, follows the whole verbal phrase:

Example:	No, **no** he visto esa película	*No, I have not seen that film*
	Ella **no** había venido **tampoco**	*She hadn't come either*
	No he recibido **ninguna** oferta	*I haven't received any offers*
	No hemos encontrado a **nadie**	*We haven't found anyone*

3. Most negatives can alternatively precede the verb, and in these cases **no** is eliminated:

Example: **Nada** se movía — ***Nothing*** *was moving*
Nunca quieres acostarte — *You* ***never*** *want to go to bed*
Ningún taxi esperaba delante de la estación
No *taxi was waiting in front of the station*
Ni mi padre **ni** mi madre quieren asistir al concierto
Neither *my father* ***nor*** *my mother want to attend the concert*

4. You can use two or more negatives in one sentence.
They can precede and/or follow the verb, in accordance with the previous rules:

Example: **Ya no** hace **nada** — *He* ***no longer*** *does* ***anything***
No quiero ver **jamás** a **nadie** — *I* ***don't*** *want to see* ***anybody ever***

A negative at the beginning of the sentence does not remove the necessity for other negatives:

the English — ***Never*** *had he insulted* ***anybody*** *on* ***any*** *occasion*
is translated as — **Jamás** había insultado a **nadie** en **ninguna** ocasión

5. If you want to use a negative with a verb in the infinitive, it surrounds the verb in the usual way:

Example: Prefiero **no** contestar — *I prefer* ***not*** *to answer*
Me preocupa **no** saber **nada** — *Knowing* ***nothing*** *worries me*
Ella ha decidido **no** decir **ni** una palabra
She has decided ***not*** *to say a single word*

Contrast these examples with:

No quiero entrar en el edificio — *I don't want to go into the building*
No podía hacerlo yo **tampoco** — *I wasn't able to do it either*

In both these instances the negation is focussed on the person "I" and not the infinitive.

6. Most negatives can be used for one-word answers: **no, nada, nadie, ninguno, nunca, jamás, apenas, tampoco**:

Example: ¿Qué compraste en la tienda? ¡**Nada**!
What did you buy in the shop? ***Nothing!***
¿A quién viste hoy? ¡A **nadie**!
Who(m) did you see today? ***Nobody****!*
¿Has ido alguna vez a esa piscina? ¡**Jamás**!
Have you ever been to that swimming-pool? ***Never!***

7. When saying or implying "no" indirectly, **que** is inserted before **no**:

Example: ¿Se debe hacer? - Digo **que no** — *Should it be done? I say "no"*
¿Ha tenido éxito? Creo **que no** — *Has he been successful? I think not*

Notice also the construction:

¿Quién quiere probarlo? ¡Yo **no**! — *Who wants to try it?* ***Not*** *me!*
¿Quieres jugar al tenis? ¡Ahora **no**! — *Do you want to play tennis?* ***Not*** *now!*
Queremos pintar el modelo ¡Aquí **no**! — *We want to paint the model.* ***Not*** *here!*

QUESTION FORMS (LAS FORMAS INTERROGATIVAS)

Formation of Questions

These are also known as Interrogatives.
There are five ways in which you can ask questions in Spanish:

1. In speaking, the tone of voice can turn a statement into a question:

   Example: ¿Te gusta el queso? *Do you like cheese?*

2. By inverting the subject and verb:

   Example: ¿Ha bebido Vd. toda la leche? *Have you drunk all the milk?*
   ¿No compró Rita el coche? *Didn't Rita buy the car?*

3. By putting **¿verdad?** or **¿no?** at the end of a sentence:

   Example: Hace frío, ¿verdad? *Isn't it cold?*
   Hace frío, ¿no? *It's cold, isn't it?*

4. By putting **¿Es que ...** or **¿Acaso ...** at the beginning of the sentence:

   Example: ¿**Es que** el sistema no funciona? *Is the system not working?*
   ¿**Acaso** el sistema no funciona? *Is the system not working?*

5. By using question words at the beginning of the sentence:

   Example: ¿**Adónde** vas esta noche? ***Where** are you going tonight?*

Some common question words are:

¿Adónde?	*Where to?*
¿Cómo?	*How? What? What is ... like?*
¿Cuál?* ¿Cuáles?*	*Which?*
¿Cuándo?	*When?*
¿Cuánto?* ¿Cuánta?*	*How much?*
¿Cuántos?* ¿Cuántas?*	*How many?*
¿Dónde?	*Where?*
¿Para qué?	*What for?*
¿Por qué?	*Why?*
¿Qué?	*What?*
¿Quién? ¿Quiénes?	*Who?*

* These can function as adjectives or pronouns. When they are adjectives they **must** agree with the noun they accompany. See Adjectives and Pronouns on pages 17 and 59-60.

Modal Verbs (Los Verbos Modales Auxiliares)

Use of Modal Verbs

There are several verbs in Spanish including **deber, poder, querer** and **saber** which need special attention.
They often need another verb to follow them, and they can have special meanings in certain tenses.
Three of them, **poder, querer** and **saber**, are also irregular, so you should check their forms in the Verb Table.

Deber

This verb has two meanings - *to owe, to have to*

When it is used in its meaning of *to owe* it functions on its own, without another verb:

Example:	Él me **debe** mil euros	*He owes me 1000 euros*
	¿Cuánto te **debo**?	*How much do I owe you?*

When **deber** means *to have to* it must have another verb to follow it in the sentence, and that verb is always in the **infinitive**.

Example:	Debo **partir**	*I have to leave, I must leave*
	Debería **irme**	*I should go*

Deber also occurs with the preposition **de**, when it usually indicates a likely supposition.

There are various shades of meaning for **deber (de)**:

1. **must** in the sense of **being obliged to**:
   Example: **Debemos** ir a la escuela
   *We **have to**/We **must**/We **have got to** go to school*

2. **must** in the sense of **something being arranged, being supposed to**:
   Example: **Debo** ir a ver a mis primos
   *I **am supposed to**/I **have to** visit my cousins*

3. **must** in the sense of a **likely supposition** or **probability**:
   Example: Bajo estas circunstancias **debe de** ser muy difícil para Vd.
   *Under these circumstances it **must** be very difficult for you*

4. In the preterite tense **deber (de)** can mean either **ought to have** (unfulfilled obligation) or **must have** (supposition):
   Example: **Debimos** ir a ver a nuestros amigos ayer
   *We **ought/were supposed to have** gone to see our friends yesterday*
   Debieron de irse sin avisarnos
   *They **must have** left without telling us*

5. In the conditional tense it can mean **should** or **ought to**:
   Example: **Debería** escribirle *I **ought to**/I **should** write to him/her*

PODER

This verb can also be used in more than one sense. It is usually used with a second verb following it and this second verb is always in the **infinitive**:

Example: Podemos **partir** a las diez *We can leave at 10 o'clock*

There are various shades of meaning for **poder**:

1. It has the meaning of **can** in the sense of **may** or **having permission to**

   Example: **Puedes** venir a verla mañana *You **can** come and see her tomorrow*

   ¿**Puedo** ayudarle a Vd.? ***May** I help you?*

2. It has the meaning of **can** in the sense of **being able to**

   Example: Él no **puede** levantar ese peso *He **can't** lift that weight*

3. It has the meaning of **may** in the sense of **it is possible**

   Example: Ella **puede** llegar esta tarde *She **may** arrive this evening*

4. In the preterite tense **poder** means **to manage to**

   Example: **Pudieron** reparar el motor *They **managed** to repair the engine*

5. In the conditional tense **poder** means **could** or **might**

   Example: ¿**Podrías** llevarme al centro? ***Could** you take me to the centre?*

   Por lo menos **podría** llamarme *He **might** at least call me*

QUERER

This verb has two meanings - *to love, to want*

When it is used with either meaning, it can function on its own, without another verb:

Example: **Queremos** a nuestros padres *We **love** our parents*

Ella **quería** una hamburguesa *She **wanted** a hamburger*

When it means *to want*, it sometimes has another verb following it in the sentence, and that verb is always in the **infinitive**.

Example: **Quiero** ir al cine *I **want** to go to the cinema*

There are various shades of meaning for **querer**:

1. In the conditional tense, it is a more polite way of saying *want* - **would like**:

   Example: **Querría** ver el modelo nuevo *I **would like** to see the new model*

2. In the preterite tense, it means **to try to** and in the negative **to refuse to**:

   Example: **Quise** abrir la puerta *I **tried** to open the door*

   No **quisieron** venir conmigo *They **refused** to come with me*

SABER

This verb has several uses:

1. It can be used on its own, without a second verb:

Example:	**Sé** su nombre y sus señas	*I **know** his/her name and address*
	¿Cómo lo **sabe** Vd.?	*How do you **know** that?*
	Él no **sabe** qué hacer	*He doesn't **know** what to do*

2. It can be used with a second verb to mean **to know how to**:

Example:	Ella **sabe** nadar	*She **can/knows how to** swim*

Compare this use with that of **poder**
Ciertos insectos **no pueden** nadar
*Certain insects **cannot** swim*
(ie are physically incapable of swimming)

This is quite different to the idea of (not) having learnt the skill, when **saber** is used.

3. In the preterite tense, it means *to find out, to realise*:

Example:	Lloré cuando **supe** la verdad	*I wept when I **found out** the truth*
	¿Cuándo **supiste** que mentía?	*When did you **realise** that he was lying?*

4. If you have to convey the idea of *to know,* it is worth remembering that the verb **conocer** also means *to know.*

Saber is used to convey the idea of *to have knowledge of* science, a language, geography, facts, etc.

Conocer conveys the idea of *being acquainted with* a person, a town, a country, a book, a film, etc.

Example: **Sé** donde está Málaga pero no **conozco** la ciudad
*I **know** where Málaga is but I don't **know** the city*
(= I have not been there)

SER AND ESTAR

Spanish has two verbs that mean *to be*: **ser** and **estar**. They are both highly irregular and their conjugation appears in the Verb Table, pages 103-107. Sometimes the English verb *to be* must be translated by **ser** because the use of **estar** would be grammatically incorrect, and sometimes the opposite is true. In addition, in certain situations **ser** and **estar** may **both** be grammatically correct but in those cases they will mean different things.

Ser tends to be used with inherent or enduring qualities (eg nationalities, professions, fundamental characteristics), while **estar** tends to be used with features which may change or end and to refer to geographical location.

Example:	Juan **es** español	*Juan is Spanish*	(he cannot stop being Spanish)
	Juan **está** descontento	*Juan is unhappy*	(he can stop being unhappy)
	María **es** abogada	*Maria is a lawyer*	(that is her profession)
	María **está** de turno	*Maria is on duty*	(a period of time that will end)
	La química **es** una asignatura compleja	*Chemistry is a complex subject*	
	El laboratorio **está** en ese edificio	*The laboratory is in that building*	

Compare the used of **ser** and **estar** in the following examples:

La manzana **es** verde	*The apple is green*	(it's green by nature, eg it's a Granny Smith)
La manzana **está** verde	*The apple is unripe*	(the apple will eventually ripen)
La hierba **es** verde	*Grass is green*	(grass is naturally, genetically green)
La hierba **está** verde	*The grass looks green*	(today the grass seems particularly green)
La hierba **está** seca	*The grass is dry*	(it's dry only until the next time it rains)
La hierba **está** amarilla	*The grass is yellow*	(it will "green up" again when it gets water)

Notice the change of meaning in the following examples when **ser** and **estar** are used:

ser aburrido	*to be bor**ing***	**estar** aburrido	*to be bor**ed***
ser consciente	*to be aware*	**estar** (in)consciente	*to be (un)conscious*
ser listo	*to be clever*	**estar** listo	*to be ready, prepared*
ser seguro	*to be safe, definite*	**estar** seguro	*to be certain, convinced*

Remember that **estar** is used with the gerund to form the continuous present tense:

estoy trabajando	*I am working*	**están** cenando	*they are dining*

Ser is also used with the past participle to form the passive, while **estar** combines with the past participle to describe a resulting state. Notice that these usages are rather different to those just described above. Compare the following examples:

El problema **fue** eliminado por el técnico	*The problem was eliminated by the technician*
Ahora el problema **está** eliminado	*Now the problem is eliminated*

(Note: In the second sentence the implication is that the problem is permanently eliminated and there is <u>no</u> suggestion that it might return.)

IMPERSONAL VERBS (LOS VERBOS IMPERSONALES)

Spanish uses many impersonal verbs (eg *It is important that, It was necessary to*)

1. **Gustar** - *to please* is probably the commonest of these. It is used to translate the English verb *to like*, so instead of saying *I like it*, in Spanish you say *It pleases me*:

Example:	Me gusta	Me gustó	Te gusta	Les gustó
	I like it	*I liked it*	*You like it*	*They liked it*

Gustar can also have a **subject**.
Instead of saying *I like ice cream*
in Spanish you say ***Ice cream*** (subject) *pleases* (verb) *me* (object pronoun)

Example:	Me gusta **el helado**	A ella le gustó **la película**	Te gustan **los deportes**
	I like ***ice cream***	*She liked* ***the film***	*You like* ***sports***

Note! In all these examples, the word order is:

1 optional **a** + prepositional pronoun (for clarification or emphasis)
2 object pronoun
3 verb
4 subject

Gustar **always** agrees with its **subject,** and is therefore to be found **only** in the third person singular or plural, agreeing for instance with ***film*** or ***sports*** as above.

The subject of **gustar** can be a **verb or verbal phrase** instead of a noun.

Example:	Os gusta **ir a la playa**	Nos gustaba **nadar en el lago**
	You (pl) like ***going to the beach***	*We used to like* ***swimming in the lake***
	(=Going to the beach pleases you)	(=Swimming in the lake used to please us)

2. The other very common impersonal verb is **haber**: **hay** (irregular invariable present tense form), **había, hubo, ha habido, habrá, habría**, etc (all regular **third person singular** forms), meaning *there is/are, there was, there will be,* etc.

Example:	**Hay** dos reuniones hoy	***There are*** *two meetings today*
	Había mucha gente en la plaza	***There were*** *many people in the square*
	Hubo varios incidentes	***There were*** *several incidents*
	Ha habido pocos intentos	***There have been*** *few attempts*
	En la fiesta **habrá** limonada	***There will be*** *lemonade at the party*

All these forms of **haber** can be combined with **que** to create a phrase implying obligation or necessity:

Example:	**Hay que** lavar el coche hoy	*The car* ***must be/ought to be*** *washed today*
	Habrá que hacer las maletas	*The suitcases* ***will have to be*** *packed*

3. There are many other impersonal verbs or verbs that can be used impersonally including: **bastar, doler, encantar, fascinar, fastidiar, hacer** (of the weather), **hacer falta, importar, interesar, molestar, precisar, sobrar**

Example:	Me **duelen** las muelas	*I have toothache* (=My teeth hurt me)
	Hace calor/fresco/frío	*It is hot/cool/cold*
	Hacía buen/mal tiempo	*It was fine/It was bad weather*
	Importa prepararse bien	*It is important to prepare oneself well*
	¿Os **molestaba** el calor?	*Were you bothered by the heat?*
	Nos **sobran** legumbres	*We have more than enough vegetables*

The Infinitive (El Infinitivo)

In addition to modal auxiliary verbs, there are many other circumstances in which a second verb (in the infinitive) is required.
The infinitive may either be placed straight after the first verb, or the first verb may require **a**, **de**, **en** or more rarely **con** or **por** between it and the infinitive.
Unfortunately, there is no easy way of knowing which method is used. You should make every effort to learn each verb + preposition (if one appears) as a **single** unit.

1. Some verbs which are followed **directly** by an infinitive include:

conseguir	*to manage to*	pedir	*to ask to*
deber	*to have to*	pensar	*to intend to*
decidir	*to decide to*	permitir	*to permit to*
desear	*to want/wish to*	poder	*to be able to*
esperar	*to hope to*	preferir	*to prefer to*
fingir	*to pretend to*	procurar	*to try to*
intentar	*to try to*	prometer	*to promise to*
jurar	*to swear to*	querer	*to wish/want to*
lograr	*to succeed in*	recordar	*to remember (to)*
merecer	*to deserve to*	saber	*to know (how to)*
necesitar	*to need to*	seguir	*to continue to*
odiar	*to hate to*	sentir	*to regret, to be sorry to/for*
ofrecer	*to offer to*	soler	*to be accustomed to*
parecer	*to seem to*	temer	*to fear to*

Example:	Ella **merece** tener éxito	*She **deserves** to be successful*
	Siento no poder ayudarte	***I am sorry** not to be able to help you*
	Él **esperaba** ganar	***He was hoping** to win*
	Ha prometido acompañarnos	***He has promised** to accompany us*

2. Some verbs which require **a + an infinitive** are:

aprender a	*to learn to*	enseñar a* alguien a	*to teach someone to*
apresurarse a	*to hurry to*	invitar a* alguien a	*to invite someone to*
atreverse a	*to dare to*	ir a	*to be going to*
ayudar a* alguien a	*to help someone to*	limitarse a	*to limit oneself to*
comenzar a	*to begin to*	negarse a	*to refuse to*
decidirse a	*to make up one's mind to*	obligar a* alguien a	*to oblige someone to*
		ponerse a	*to begin/start to*
disponerse a	*to get ready to*	prepararse a	*to prepare oneself to*
empezar a	*to begin to*	resignarse a	*to resign oneself to*

Example:	Ella está enseñando a su hijo **a** leer	*She is teaching her son to read*
	Se pusieron **a** cavar	*They set about digging*
	Ella se niega **a** bailar	*She refuses to dance*
	Empieza **a** llover	*It's beginning to rain*
	Invitaron a los García **a** cenar	*They invited the Garcías to supper*

* The "a" before alguien is in all cases the personal "a". See page 43.

3. Some verbs which require **de + infinitive** are:

acordarse de	*to remember*	desesperar de	*to despair of*
arrepentirse de	*to regret*	encargarse de	*to take responsibility for*
cansarse de	*to become tired of*	hartarse de	*to have enough of,*
cesar de	*to stop, cease from*		*to become sick of*
cuidar de	*to take care of*	terminar de	*to finish*
dejar de	*to stop, give up*	tratar de	*to try to*

Example: Me encargué **de** organizar la fiesta — *I undertook to organise the party*
Trataré **de** llamarte mañana — *I shall try to call you tomorrow*

4. Some verbs which require **en + infinitive** are:

consentir en	*to consent to*	insistir en	*to insist on*
consistir en	*to consist of*	persistir en	*to persist in*
convenir en	*to agree to*	quedar en	*to agree to*
divertirse en	*to amuse oneself by*	tardar en	*to be late in,*
dudar en	*to have doubts about,*		*to be a long time in*
	to hesitate to/over	vacilar en	*to hesitate to/over*

Example: Dudaba **en** comprar el traje
He was having doubts about buying the suit
Tardaron mucho **en** traernos la cuenta
They were a long time in bringing us the bill

5. A few verbs require either **con + infinitive** or **por + infinitive**:

amenazar con	*to threaten to*	decidirse por	*to decide on/upon, to choose*
contar con	*to count on*	interesarse por	*to take an interest in*
soñar con	*to dream of*	optar por	*to opt for*

Example: Soñé **con** matar dragones — *I dreamt of killing dragons*
Optamos **por** tomar el tren — *We opted to take the train*

6. Expressions with **tener** which are followed by **de + infinitive**:

Example:

tener ganas de	**Tengo ganas de** comer fresas
to want to/feel like	***I want to** eat/**I feel like** eating strawberries*
tener la gentileza de	Ella **tuvo la gentileza de** prestarme el libro
to be kind enough to	*She **was kind enough to** lend me the book*
tener miedo de	**Tenían miedo de** salir por la noche
to be afraid to	***They were afraid to** go out at night*

7. **Para** can also be used to introduce an infinitive and gives the meaning of *to, in order to*:

Example: Eres demasiado joven **para** conducir
*You are too young **to** drive*
Ella fue al supermercado **para** comprar azúcar
*She went to the supermarket **in order to** buy some sugar*

8. **Antes de** *before*, **después de** *after*, **en lugar de** *instead of*, **hasta** *until*, **nada más** *as soon as*, **por** *through, from*, **sin** *without* may all be followed by an infinitive:

Example: Ella siguió **hasta** no poder más
*She continued **until** she could do so no longer*
Después de empezar, pero **antes de** terminar, deberías hacer una pausa
***After** beginning but **before** finishing you should take a break*
En lugar de quedarnos decidimos partir **sin decir** adónde íbamos
***Instead** of staying we decided to leave **without saying** where we were going*

9. **Al** + infinitive gives the sense of *on, while, when, upon, just as, by* doing something:

Example: **Al verme**, se fue apresuradamente
***On/Upon** seeing me, he left in a hurry*
Llegó Enrique **al dar** las doce
*Enrique arrived **just as** it was striking twelve*
Al detenerse el autobús, todos intentaron subir a la vez
***When the bus stopped** they all tried to get on at the same time*

OTHER FACTS ABOUT VERBS (OTROS DATOS SOBRE LOS VERBOS)

1. Notice these special constructions with: **mandar, obligar a, permitir, prohibir**. (all verbs of ordering, allowing or forbidding). They need the object pronoun or personal "a" + noun with the infinitive:

Example:	Ella **le mandó** limpiar su habitación	***She ordered him*** *to clean his room*
	¿Me obligarás a acompañarte?	***Will you make me*** *accompany you?*
	Permiten a su hijo salir solo	***They let their son*** *go out alone*
	He prohibido a Juan llamarme	***I have forbidden Juan*** *to phone me*

2. In Spanish there is **no** preposition after these verbs even though one is needed in English:

aguardar	*to wait **for***	buscar	*to look **for***
escuchar	*to listen **to***	esperar	*to wait **for***
mirar	*to look **at***	pagar	*to pay **for***
pedir	*to ask **for***		

Example:	**Miramos** los animales	*We look **at** the animals*
	Escuchaba la radio	*I was listening **to** the radio*
	Estoy buscando los libros	*I'm looking **for** the books*
	Estoy buscando a los niños*	*I'm looking **for** the children*
	Pedimos tres limonadas	*We asked **for** three lemonades*

*Note the personal "a".

3. The following constructions are worthy of note.
They need **a** for the person and the word order is different from the English

- dar algo **a** alguien — Doy dinero **a** mi hermano
  I give my brother some money
- enviar algo **a** alguien — Ella envía una carta **a** su hermana
  She sends her sister a letter
- mostrar algo **a** alguien — Muestro el mapa **a** mi padre
  I show my father the map
- prestar algo **a** alguien — ¿Prestaste tu abrigo **a** Pablo?
  Did you lend Pablo your overcoat?

4. The preposition following the verb in these sentences is also **a**.
Here it means ***for*** or ***from***:

- Pedí el número de teléfono **a** la señora
  *I asked the lady **for** the phone number*
- Ha comprado unas manzanas **a** la granjera
  *He has bought some apples **from** the farmer's wife*
- Pedimos prestado el coche **a** mi tío
  *We borrowed the car **from** my uncle*
- El niño robó los dulces **a** su hermana
  *The little boy stole the sweets **from** his sister*

5. Other verbs requiring **a** include:

• acercarse **a**	Me acerqué **al** hotel *I approached/went up to the hotel*
• acostumbrarse **a**	Voy acostumbrándome **a** la nueva dieta *I am gradually getting used to the new diet*
• asistir **a**	Asistiremos **a** la ceremonia mañana *We shall attend the ceremony tomorrow*
• jugar **a**	Ella juega **al** hockey *She plays hockey*
• parecerse **a**	Te pareces **a** tu padre *You are like your father*
• salir **a**	Mi hermana sale **a** su abuelo *My sister takes after her grandfather*
• tocar **a**	Toco muchas piezas **al** piano *I play a lot of pieces on the piano*
but	Toco la guitarra *I play the guitar*

6. Some verbs requiring other prepositions:

• acordarse **de**	Me acuerdo **de** los cumpleaños de mis amigos *I remember my friends' birthdays*
• pensar **de**	¿Qué piensas **de** mi traje nuevo? *What do you think of my new suit?*
• pensar **en**	Ella pensaba **en** la lección de hoy *She was thinking about today's lesson*

7. There are a number of useful idioms that use the verb **tener**:

• tener	¿Qué tiene Vd.? No tengo nada *Is something the matter?* *Nothing's the matter with me*
• tener hambre/sed	Tengo sed pero curiosamente no tengo hambre *I'm thirsty but curiously I'm not hungry*
• tener calor/frío	Tienes calor ahora pero tendrás frío más tarde *You're hot now but you'll be/feel cold later*
• tener **que**	Tengo que practicar una hora todos los días *I must/have to practise for an hour every day*

WORD ORDER (EL ORDEN DE LAS PALABRAS)

Word order in Spanish is fairly similar to English word order, but there are certain differences which you must know:

1. The biggest difference is the position of the **subject** relative to the **verb**. In English we always say *The customers complain* but in Spanish you can say **either** Los clientes se quejan **or** Se quejan los clientes, and whichever element comes **second** (subject or verb) is the idea that is particularly stressed.

   When there is also an object in the sentence, there is still a good deal of flexibility.

You can say:	Laura come la manzana	*Laura eats the apple*
or	Come Laura la manzana	
or	Come la manzana Laura	

   though the second and third possibilities are much less common in everyday language.

2. **Personal pronouns** are placed before their verb, except when they are attached to the end of infinitives, gerunds and positive commands.
   Given the behaviour of the subject in Spanish, it is very common to find sentences that follow the order:

   1 object pronoun
   2 verb
   3 subject

   Example: Lo vendió Pablo *Pablo sold it*

   With impersonal verbs this is the **standard** word order:
   Example: Me encantan las joyas *I love jewels*

   See Pronouns especially pages 53 - 54
   See Impersonal Verbs pages 96

3. Most **adjectives** come after the noun.
   See Adjectives especially pages 11 - 12

4. **Adverbs** tend to follow their verb, either the single word in simple tenses or the verbal phrase in compound tenses.
   Do **not** put adverbs between the auxiliary and the past participle.
   See Adverbs especially page 20

5. You should take care with the position of the **negatives,** as these can precede, come before **and** after, or just follow the verb.
   See Negatives pages 89 - 90

6. Remember that **questions** can be asked by inverting the subject and verb. When there is also an object the normal word order is
   verb - subject - object.
   See Questions page 91

Verb Table

Infinitivo **Infinitive**	**Presente** **Present**	**Pretérito Indefinido** **Preterite**	**Pretérito Imperfecto** **Imperfect**	**Futuro** **Future**	**Subjuntivo Presente** **Present Subjunctive**
andar *to walk,* *to go*	ando andas anda andamos andáis andan	anduve anduviste anduvo anduvimos anduvisteis anduvieron	andaba andabas andaba andábamos andabais andaban	andaré andarás andará andaremos andaréis andarán	ande andes ande andemos andéis anden
caber *to fit*	quepo cabes cabe cabemos cabéis caben	cupe cupiste cupo cupimos cupisteis cupieron	cabía cabías cabía cabíamos cabíais cabían	cabré cabrás cabrá cabremos cabréis cabrán	quepa quepas quepa quepamos quepáis quepan
dar *to give*	doy das da damos dais dan	di diste dio dimos disteis dieron	daba dabas daba dábamos dabais daban	daré darás dará daremos daréis darán	dé des dé demos deis den
decir *to say*	digo dices dice decimos decís dicen	dije dijiste dijo dijimos dijisteis dijeron	decía decías decía decíamos decíais decían	diré dirás dirá diremos diréis dirán	diga digas diga digamos digáis digan

Verb Table

Infinitivo Infinitive	Presente Present	Pretérito Indefinido Preterite	Pretérito Imperfecto Imperfect	Futuro Future	Subjuntivo Presente Present Subjunctive
estar *to be*	estoy estás está estamos estáis están	estuve estuviste estuvo estuvimos estuvisteis estuvieron	estaba estabas estaba estábamos estabais estaban	estaré estarás estará estaremos estaréis estarán	esté estés esté estemos estéis estén
haber *to have* (auxiliary)	he has ha hemos habéis han	hube hubiste hubo hubimos hubisteis hubieron	había habías había habíamos habíais habían	habré habrás habrá habremos habréis habrán	haya hayas haya hayamos hayáis hayan
hacer *to do,* *to make*	hago haces hace hacemos hacéis hacen	hice hiciste hizo hicimos hicisteis hicieron	hacía hacías hacía hacíamos hacíais hacían	haré harás hará haremos haréis harán	haga hagas haga hagamos hagáis hagan
ir *to go*	voy vas va vamos vais van	fui fuiste fue fuimos fuisteis fueron	iba ibas iba íbamos ibais iban	iré irás irá iremos iréis irán	vaya vayas vaya vayamos vayáis vayan

Verb Table

Infinitivo Infinitive	Presente Present	Pretérito Indefinido Preterite	Pretérito Imperfecto Imperfect	Futuro Future	Subjuntivo Presente Present Subjunctive
oír *to hear*	oigo oyes oye oímos oís oyen	oí oíste oyó oímos oísteis oyeron	oía oías oía oíamos oíais oían	oiré oirás oirá oiremos oiréis oirán	oiga oigas oiga oigamos oigáis oigan
poder *to be able to*	puedo puedes puede podemos podéis pueden	pude pudiste pudo pudimos pudisteis pudieron	podía podías podía podíamos podíais podían	podré podrás podrá podremos podréis podrán	pueda puedas pueda podamos podáis puedan
poner *to put*	pongo pones pone ponemos ponéis ponen	puse pusiste puso pusimos pusisteis pusieron	ponía ponías ponía poníamos poníais ponían	pondré pondrás pondrá pondremos pondréis pondrán	ponga pongas ponga pongamos pongáis pongan
querer *to wish,* *to want,* *to love*	quiero quieres quiere queremos queréis quieren	quise quisiste quiso quisimos quisisteis quisieron	quería querías quería queríamos queríais querían	querré querrás querrá querremos querréis querrán	quiera quieras quiera queramos queráis quieran

Verb Table

Infinitivo Infinitive	Presente Present	Pretérito Indefinido Preterite	Pretérito Imperfecto Imperfect	Futuro Future	Subjuntivo Presente Present Subjunctive
reír *to laugh*	río ríes ríe reímos reís ríen	reí reíste rió reímos reísteis rieron	reía reías reía reíamos reíais reían	reiré reirás reirá reiremos reiréis reirán	ría rías ría riamos riáis rían
saber *to know*	sé sabes sabe sabemos sabéis saben	supe supiste supo supimos supisteis supieron	sabía sabías sabía sabíamos sabíais sabían	sabré sabrás sabrá sabremos sabréis sabrán	sepa sepas sepa sepamos sepáis sepan
salir *to go out*	salgo sales sale salimos salís salen	salí saliste salió salimos salisteis salieron	salía salías salía salíamos salíais salían	saldré saldrás saldrá saldremos saldréis saldrán	salga salgas salga salgamos salgáis salgan
satisfacer *to satisfy*	satisfago satisfaces satisface satisfacemos satisfacéis satisfacen	satisfice satisficiste satisfizo satisficimos satisficisteis satisficieron	satisfacía satisfacías satisfacía satisfacíamos satisfacíais satisfacían	satisfaré satisfarás satisfará satisfaremos satisfaréis satisfarán	satisfaga satisfagas satisfaga satisfagamos satisfagáis satisfagan

Verb Table

Infinitivo Infinitive	Presente Present	Pretérito Indefinido Preterite	Pretérito Imperfecto Imperfect	Futuro Future	Subjuntivo Presente Present Subjunctive
ser	soy	fui	era	seré	sea
to be	eres	fuiste	eras	serás	seas
	es	fue	era	será	sea
	somos	fuimos	éramos	seremos	seamos
	sois	fuisteis	erais	seréis	seáis
	son	fueron	eran	serán	sean
tener	tengo	tuve	tenía	tendré	tenga
to have	tienes	tuviste	tenías	tendrás	tengas
	tiene	tuvo	tenía	tendrá	tenga
	tenemos	tuvimos	teníamos	tendremos	tengamos
	tenéis	tuvisteis	teníais	tendréis	tengáis
	tienen	tuvieron	tenían	tendrán	tengan
venir	vengo	vine	venía	vendré	venga
to come	vienes	viniste	venías	vendrás	vengas
	viene	vino	venía	vendrá	venga
	venimos	vinimos	veníamos	vendremos	vengamos
	venís	vinisteis	veníais	vendréis	vengáis
	vienen	vinieron	venían	vendrán	vengan
ver	veo	vi	veía	veré	vea
to see	ves	viste	veías	verás	veas
	ve	vio	veía	verá	vea
	vemos	vimos	veíamos	veremos	veamos
	veis	visteis	veíais	veréis	veáis
	ven	vieron	veían	verán	vean

Index